Inspiring Meaningful Learning

6 STEPS TO CREATING LESSONS THAT ENGAGE
STUDENTS IN DEEP LEARNING

Brenda Stein Dzaldov

Pembroke Publishers Limited

As always, to Jenny, Mitch, and Benji and, of course, Ophir.
I love you.

© 2018 Pembroke Publishers
538 Hood Road
Markham, Ontario, Canada L3R 3K9
www.pembrokepublishers.com

Distributed in the U.S. by Stenhouse Publishers
www.stenhouse.com

Funded by the Government of Canada
Financé par le gouvernement du Canada | Canadä

Ontario
Ontario Media Development Corporation
Société de développement de l'industrie des médias de l'Ontario

---

Library and Archives Canada Cataloguing in Publication

Dzaldov, Brenda Stein, author
    Inspiring meaningful learning : 6 steps to creating lessons that engage students in deep learning / Brenda Stein Dzaldov.

Includes index.
Issued in print and electronic formats.
ISBN 978-1-55138-334-7 (softcover).—ISBN 978-1-55138-934-9 (PDF)

    1. Lesson planning. 2. Learning. I. Title.

LB1027.4.D93 2018   371.3028   C2018-903293-6
                                   C2018-903294-4

Editor: Kat Mototsune
Cover Design: John Zehethofer
Typesetting: Jay Tee Graphics Ltd.

Printed and bound in Canada
9 8 7 6 5 4 3 2 1

Contents

Introduction

As teachers, you work hard. You spend your days with students and colleagues, teaching, learning, coaching, supporting, assessing, communicating, building relationships, and much more. Then, when the instructional day is finished, you go home and spend time planning for the next day or week. There are multiple levels of planning required: long-range planning to map out the year; unit planning to organize instructional blocks by content or theme; planning to keep track of the daily schedule and agenda; and, of course, lesson planning to create experiences that will not only engage students in learning but also make learning exciting, meaningful, interesting, and permanent!

The thought, development, and preparation you put into designing many lessons every day is extraordinary, as you work to find ways to structure lessons that affect learning and engage students in meaningful learning experiences. Therefore, it is crucial to have a format for lesson planning that supports a practical yet inspiring approach to teaching and learning.

Throughout my career, one of the most important things I learned is that planning is necessary for meaningful learning. Knowing and connecting with your students, both academically and personally, is a starting point. Knowing your curriculum is next. Knowing approaches for teaching and learning, such as inclusive pedagogy, differentiated instruction, universal design for learning, cooperative learning, inquiry-based learning, and many more, starts with good planning. As an educator, I have spent many years developing lessons and planning at many levels and, over time, I have seen how an organized, practical lesson design, backed by the theory around what educators know about engagement, motivation, and learning, can make our jobs much easier and truly fulfilling—because meaningful learning ensues.

I have known for many years that content knowledge is crucial in teaching and learning. Before we can teach, we need to learn content deeply. We need to know *what* we are teaching, and planning supports that. I have taught everything from the water cycle, to how to do a bounce pass in physical education (not my most stellar moment!), to a wide range of approaches to understanding fractions. And I can confidently say that I knew the content well, and my students benefited from this. It allowed me to plan to teach flexibly, to facilitate learning, to promote good discussions, and to ask and respond to questions that support deep thinking.

At the same time, you need a toolkit of instructional strategies you can use to engage in the *how* to teach that best supports learning. Planning the best pedagogical approach that supports as many learners as possible is easier when you know about a wide range of available pedagogies. Is it better to try this activity using an organizer? Is it best to give students choice in this lesson? Can students suggest the text to use for this task? Can all students benefit from using a specific technology in this lesson? Should I spend more time on small-group work or move quickly to one-on-one conferences? All these questions will come up in your regular planning, and when you have the tools to answer these questions meaningfully, you can truly support students in their learning.

Finally, I have seen that rapport matters tremendously. In fact, rapport needs to be a focus in planning too. Too many times I have seen how harsh words, sarcasm, or a lack of connection can turn students off engaged learning. In contrast, I have watched how kindness, caring, and connection have changed the landscape for students and their teachers. I distinctly remember working with a Grade 3 teacher. A student walked in late, his head down, shuffling his feet. The teacher was at the front of the class, in the middle of a lesson. She turned toward the student with a smile, looked him in the eye, and said, "Welcome, Jay! We've been waiting for you and we're so glad you're here." The student's demeanor instantly changed from downcast to cheerful and he moved quickly to get his learning materials and join the class with a smile on his face. In that moment I saw how welcoming students into our classrooms, demonstrating a quick caring moment, and making a connection can change the way students look at learning.

Inspiring Meaningful Learning is based on a lesson design that engages students in learning, one that integrates content, pedagogy, and rapport to provide an organized, comprehensive way to plan lessons that inspire kids to want to learn. It reminds you each day to connect to your students, share content, and choose appropriate pedagogies that encourage students to question, practice, self-assess, and collaborate in a safe, comfortable environment created by you and your students. It transfers some of the responsibility for student learning to the student, creating an atmosphere for self-regulation, self-assessment, and engagement. As you get into the rhythm of lesson design within the backdrop of meaningful learning, you will see your practices change. You will experience the wonderful feeling of seeing your students deeply engaged in their own thinking, doing, and learning.

I have been a teacher for more than 25 years, and I know some things for sure about teaching and learning. I know that content is important, that well-chosen pedagogies can be very engaging and supportive of student learning, and that, if rapport is present, teaching and learning is happier, easier, more engaging, and more meaningful for both teachers and students. I also know that planning for instruction can create meaningful learning experiences that consciously incorporate all three of these important aspects of learning into daily lessons. Of course, educators can't be perfect. We do our best to incorporate all areas of meaningful learning into every lesson, but time can be short, or the unexpected happens, and it is sometimes necessary for us to make instructional decisions that are best for our students by recalibrating, adding, or deleting parts of lessons. Use the six steps presented in this book to inspire meaningful learning through lesson design; fill your toolkit with ideas and activities that you will use as needed and based on the needs of your students. Try them one by one and evaluate the difference they make to your relationship with your students and to student learning. I'm certain you will be pleased with the results. When your students thank you, ask deep questions, share feedback, and exclaim, "I get it!" "This makes sense!" or "Now I know why we're learning this!" you will know that you have inspired meaningful learning in your students. And that is the best feeling of all for any teacher.

How to Plan for Meaningful Learning

"When I was a student, I used to try to learn the way teachers taught, but now I teach the way students learn."

— *Emma, first-year Grade 6 teacher*

In more than 25 years of working with teachers, both new and experienced, I have found that two important areas make for deep and meaningful learning:

1. Content Knowledge: the level of the teacher's knowledge in a given subject or content area. Teachers have to know a lot to teach meaningfully.
2. Pedagogy: a clear understanding of how students learn, individually and collaboratively, and of how to choose and implement appropriate instructional strategies. Teachers need a toolkit of strategies to use in any given teaching–learning situation.

The work of Lee Shulman (1986) refers to pedagogy and content knowledge as the two key areas teachers need to master to influence learning. This mastery results in pedagogical content knowledge, a type of knowledge unique to teachers that integrates the two areas fundamental to teaching expertise.

I would add the third crucial area to Shulman's model: rapport.

3. Rapport: a positive relationship or connection that is essential to a classroom where students are inspired to learn. When teachers and their students have this positive relationship, learning becomes more enjoyable and meaningful. The teacher who has rapport with their students is liked and respected by them, and the students are understood and liked by their teacher.

When building rapport, teachers must demonstrate these basic attitudes:

- they care about students and their learning
- they are aware of student needs and interests, and do their best to incorporate them into lesson design

— be prepared

— have a plan

— develop a relationship

- they are enthusiastic about learning
- they provide students with whole-class/small-group/one-on-one attention based on student needs
- they treat students with fairness and (equity)
- they don't break promises without explaining their reasoning

Think of that teacher you had in school, the one you liked, respected, and trusted, the one who knew the content and had interesting, meaningful, and well-organized ways of presenting the learning. We have all had those teachers. They are the ones who make a difference for us as students, the ones we learn the most from.

When students enjoy going to school, it's usually because they have favorite teachers. Students will often talk about their favorite teachers outside of school. I have asked hundreds of students about the qualities of their favorite teachers because I have always believed that the answer would provide the magic formula for new and experienced teachers to know how to create a classroom connection that makes students want to be part of learning.

The answers from students can be grouped as follows:

- The teacher notices me.
- The teacher cares about me.
- The teacher is nice (and funny, but not sarcastic).
- The teacher doesn't yell at or embarrass me.
- The teacher communicates with me in a clear way.
- I never feel afraid to ask the teacher questions.
- The teacher checks in with me to make sure I'm okay.
- The teacher cares if I'm learning.

All these answers are connected to the ideas of establishing connection or rapport. Rapport is defined as *a close and harmonious relationship in which the people or groups concerned understand each other's feelings or ideas and communicate well*. The students' answers mirror this definition of rapport, which includes how people feel and how they communicate.

Rapport is essential. Building rapport occurs throughout all the time a teacher interacts with students. However, first and foremost, it is important to notice students when they enter the classroom or learning space. For decades, teachers have been asked to stand at the classroom door and greet students as they arrive. Teachers are often busy organizing lessons, moving from room to room, speaking to an individual student or colleague before class begins. So remember that greeting students upon entry is still an excellent first way to establish rapport, but it is certainly not the only way.

Without rapport, content knowledge and good instructional strategies may not be enough to engage students in meaningful learning. Therefore, teachers must understand these three areas as necessary—and overlapping—in order to successfully plan for meaningful learning.

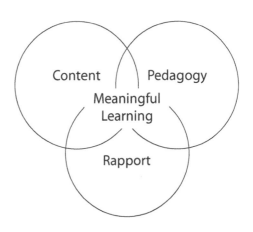

Principles of Meaningful Learning

When planning for meaningful learning, there are a number of principles that will be part of each teaching decision and that address content, pedagogy, and rapport in any lesson.

Share the Stage

Teachers are crucially important; however, teachers, teaching assistants, and other professionals are not the only ones in the classroom who hold knowledge or who can share this knowledge with others. Technology, peers, and students themselves can, of course, drive interests, goals, practice, feedback, and assessment. As knowledgeable others participate in the construction of content using relevant pedagogies, trust will ensue. Making use of these options is vitally important to creating great lessons. The more you feel able to "share the stage" with learners, the more meaningful and inspiring learning will be.

Share the Choosing of Texts

There is a wide range of texts/resources that support learning. The definition of *text* has changed from referring to only a book or other written or print artifact to representing the wide range of audio, visual, digital, and multimodal texts that abound in our world and the world of our students. David Booth shares this reflection on text:

> Today we should be concerned less with understanding one type of written text than with mastering multiple texts and modes, and the practices implied in each. We need to concentrate less on the purely linguistic and more on the multi-modal. (Booth, 2008)

Even in the past, when choices of text were more limited, the challenge has always been to choose texts/resources carefully. The challenge, its scope, and its rewards are proportionally larger now that teachers use print, digital text, apps, videos, and linear and non-linear texts on a regular basis, with both teachers and students having instant access to these multimodal texts. It is important to consider the following when planning learning with texts of all sorts:

- Including students in the choice process where possible; giving them the option to use texts that meet their interests
- Choosing the best texts to support content teaching; using a wide variety of multimodal texts.
- Teaching critical skills that support each student's interaction with text to create the most meaning possible.
- Creating space in your classroom to talk about texts; showing students that you are interested in their text choices and their thinking about the texts they read and write.

Share the Secret

It is important that the goals of the lesson and the criteria for success do not exist only on the pages of the lesson plan. Students need to know what you are teaching, what they are supposed to be learning, and what they need to know and be able to do to be successful. When students are aware of what they are learning and the criteria for success, they can become partners in the learning process by monitoring their own progress toward the goals; this results in relevant learning experiences for students.

Share the Importance

relate content to them

You need to make learning relevant to students by constantly digging deeply into students' interests and background knowledge. We know that when students' interests are engaged, their motivation to learn is increased. Sometimes a student's stake in the lesson is easy to predict; sometimes it is very individualized. Research shows that if students do not see the connection between themselves and the learning activity, they might disengage entirely in response (Fredericks, Blumenfeld & Paris, 2004). So you need to ensure that content is connected to prior knowledge and experience, making the learning meaningful in personally relevant ways.

Share Talk

Practice and encourage classroom talk that engages and motivates your students to participate and learn. There are a number of approaches that encourage talk and participation in the classroom and lead to meaningful learning:

- Don't single out students to speak in a large group; wait for them to volunteer.
- In small groups, give students a chance to express opinions and share knowledge only when they are comfortable.
- Encourage talk with prompts that are less about correct answers and more about ideas:

  - *Can you tell me more about your thinking?*
  - *What in the text made you think this?*
  - *What do others think about _____'s idea?*
  - *Can anyone add to _____'s thinking?*
  - *Do you agree or disagree with ___'s idea? Why?*
  - *What questions would you like to ask _____?*

Share the World

Incorporate the global community into your classroom. If something important is happening down the street or across the continent and kids are talking about it, do what you can to incorporate it into their learning. That means that, as a teacher, you need to stay in touch with the world through reading, listening, talking, and challenging/confirming opinions, facts, and observations. Only by doing this can you guide the learning of your students in the real world, and connect it to their world.

Planning for Meaningful Learning

The term *meaningful learning* stands in opposition to *rote learning*. Meaningful learning occurs when new knowledge is related to previous knowledge; whereas rote learning involves memorizing discrete information and facts based on repetition. When engaged in meaningful learning, students are actively learning and involved, rather than passively receiving information.

All teachers want to plan meaningful, engaging lessons. What is meaningful learning? You can be the best dictionary in this case. You know when a lesson goes well. In a successful lesson, students are engaged in learning; they are excited about learning; learning is meaningful and students achieve. There is no greater feeling than implementing a lesson that engenders meaningful learning! The question is, how can you plan this type of experience on a daily basis?

Once a topic is chosen, all modes of communication can be used to teach these concepts during the lesson. Students can engage with hands-on learning and use digital, print, visual, auditory, and multilingual texts to learn about the content and the world in meaningful ways.

> **MEANINGFUL TOPICS**
>
> In some cases, topics for lesson planning are obvious. Some topics are generally engaging for particular age groups. For example, most Kindergarten students like learning about animals. They will enjoy watching videos, making animals out of materials such as play clay, pipe cleaners, and craft sticks, and learning about animals in math and science. Many Grade 4 students have an interest in rocks and minerals; they will enjoy making rock candy out of sugar and water, and will engage with learning about various kinds of rocks and minerals such as gems, countertop stone, fossil, and lava. Most Grade 8 students will enjoy a science experiment with a "cool" result, such as experimenting with the combining of different liquids in a unit on States of Matter.

Planning the Meaningful Lesson

Any lesson has many elements: academic and curricular expectations; assessment and evaluation components; social goals; learning skills integrated into the lesson; a wide range of resources or texts to consider; traditional and new literacies to integrate; the process of integrating digital learning to give access to a wide range of resources, perspectives, and knowledge. It may sometimes seem like one teacher can't possibly do it all.

But there is a lot you can do every day and during every lesson to provide inspiring, meaningful learning opportunities for your students. It starts with an understanding of the essential components of lesson design and using that understanding as an inspiration for meaningful learning. <u>Meaningful learning happens when learners</u>

- are interested in the content
- are curious
- encounter a challenge — *whatever that is for them (equity)*
- figure out something and feel competent
- explore new information
- are aware of what they are learning and why they are learning it
- understand what they need to know and be able to do to be successful
- create a product that meaningfully demonstrates their learning

The Ideal Amount of Detail

It is tempting to create long, detailed lesson plans in hopes of supporting learners. However, such lesson plans tend to put too much of the load for all aspects of teaching and learning on the teacher. They are often too centred on whole-class teaching and make it difficult to set the stage for understanding the elements of meaningful learning.

SAMPLE OF A TEACHER-CENTRED LESSON PLAN

Dates: *Thursday, February 6* *Friday, February 7* Grade: *SK*		Title of Lesson: *Literacy – What is in your hat?*
Specific Expectation(s): *4.4 begin to use classroom resources to support their writing* *4.3 write simple messages using a combination of pictures, symbols, knowledge of the correspondence between letters and sounds (phonics), and familiar words* *4.2 demonstrate an awareness that writing can convey ideas or messages*		Learning Goal: *We are learning to write about what is in our hat using the sight word "in."*
Timing (mins)	Lesson Breakdown	
5	Pre-teaching: • *The week before we read the book,* The Mitten *by Jan Brett* • *Students have dramatized the story, recalled the animals in the story, created lists, mittens, and puppets to go inside the mitten.* • *I will have already read the students the book,* The Hat *by Jan Brett. We will have compared the differences and similarities between the two books through a Venn diagram.*	

	• *Students will be retelling the story in the library. They will be given the book* The Hat, *cards of the characters, and clothesline and clothespins to hang up the cards.*
10	Initializing: Mental Set *Students will be called by color groups to my table. We will brainstorm together ideas of what could be inside our hat, and I will record on chart paper.*
50	Sustaining: • *The writing utensils will be prepared on the table.* • *Students will go get their word rings from their individual drawers.* • *I will review the sight-word ring with each student.* • *Students will receive their sheet with their picture on it wearing their hat and a box to draw a picture of what is inside their hat.* • *Some students who are able to write independently using their sight-word ring and stretch words will begin to write "In my hat is…"* • *Some students will use their word ring, copy teacher's print, and stretch the final word with teacher support.* • *Some students will have a sheet for which they need to only fill in the word "in" and what they choose to be in their hat. I will guide students who still struggle with letter formation through each individual letter formation.* • *Throughout this process I will give descriptive feedback, letting them know a star and step.*

Success Criteria Linked to Learning Goal:
1. Students will decide what is inside their hat by using their imagination.
2. Students will use finger spaces between their words.

Questions for Higher-Level Thinking:
• *Can you describe how your hat feels and what is inside your hat?*
• *How would you feel inside a hat?*
• *Can you recall the characters from* The Hat? *What did they do when they saw Hedgie in the hat?*
• *Why do you think the other animals put on the hat?*

Assessment:
Anecdotal notes on
• *Students' ability to come up with an idea of what is inside their hat. Did they participate in brainstorming? Did they come up with an original idea or try to use someone's idea?*
• *Analyze students' letter formation and finger spaces.*
• *Observe if they are able to use resources to write words (word ring).*
• *Observe students' ability to hear letter sounds in the word they have come up with. Being able to stretch the word and record the letter sounds.*
• *Analyze fine motor skills and pencil grip.*

Accommodations:
- *For CM, JO, AB, AD I will have letter cards to help with their formation. I will guide them on the correct letter formation and focus on pencil grip.*
- *Review his name JO. I will have sandpaper letters for him to trace over with his finger.*
- *Will place MG in close proximity so she can hear me.*
- *For students who struggle with the letter formation pipe cleaners, popsicle sticks, chalk boards and letter magnet board will be available for them to make the word.*
- *I will write the word for those who need the visual aid.*
- *I will have highlighters for those who cannot write the word below and still need to trace.*

A lot of work went into this lesson design. Giving the lesson a title and including question prompts, as well as planning for assessment, are signs of effective lesson planning. There are elements in the lesson design that are clear. However, when we take a closer look, we realize certain problems:

- The teacher takes ownership for almost all the teaching and learning, and is the main source of information and feedback during classroom instruction.
- The learning goal is phrased according to what the students will do. It is not placed in a larger context for learning and doesn't make it clear why learning this is important or meaningful for students.
- The success criteria are already constructed, and they are not phrased from the perspective of the student. The success criteria seem to be more focused on task completion than on how students will demonstrate what they know and are able to do.
- The teacher has chosen all instructional approaches and activities; the onus for ensuring learning/assessment is on the teacher at all times.
- There is no input or modelling in the lesson; i.e., it is missing the time when the teacher teaches content or skills explicitly, supporting students in understanding new content and how the success criteria work in practice.
- There is no clear planning for guided/independent instruction or practice.
- Questioning is mostly closed, with correct answers expected, and follow a teacher–to-class paradigm; i.e., the teacher initiates discussion by asking a question of the whole class, waits for one student to respond, then evaluates the response with a comment (e.g., "good" or "not quite'). This Initiation–Response–Evaluation (IRE) paradigm is too often the main source of communication between teachers and students in some classrooms.
- There is no closure in this lesson design, so the students are not afforded the opportunity to share or reflect at the end of the lesson.
- This lesson design must be regenerated from scratch each time it is used, which can be arduous work for the teacher.

Other teachers use lesson plans that are more like day plans and that help them organize their resources and materials.

SAMPLE OF THE OPEN LESSON PLAN

Period	Monday	Tuesday
Week #	Monday _____ - Friday _____	
Period 1: 8:50-10:10	HW:	HW:
Period 2: 10:15-11:35	HW:	HW:
Lunch 11:35-12:10		
Period 3: 12:15-1:35	HW:	HW:
Period 4: 1:40-3:00	HW:	HW:

This kind of plan might help keep a teacher's days organized, but does not include the elements that lead to the type of meaningful learning we all aspire to in our classrooms.

Some of the main areas to consider when planning for meaningful learning are

- The role of the teacher, student, peers, and the environment and materials in engaging students in meaningful learning
- Which materials and resources (print, digital, human, and text) are most supportive and meaningful in the context of the lesson
- Student understanding of goals for learning and criteria for success in order to promote student-involved assessment (assessment as learning)
- Strategies for listening to and prompting students to understand their authentic connections, current interests, and prior knowledge
- Prompts, questions, and conversations that promote engagement, thinking, and dialogue
- Thinking beyond the walls of the classroom to support students in making meaning with the content and skills being taught

Six Steps of Meaningful Learning

Start by thinking about times in your life when you chose to learn, when you committed to learning something meaningful to you. What happened? Let's take the example of learning how to use an app.

You were **welcomed into** learning. You saw or experienced something or saw content that let you know about something to learn: a description of the app, an advertisement for it, a conversation with a friend who uses it. There was a **hook** that sparked your curiosity or directed your attention toward learning. It might have been based on a need or an interest; e.g., you want to figure out a way to access apps on organization, or you've decided to learn to use a particular app because it will help you become more organized.

Next, you set **goals** to chart a path for your learning; you figured out **what you need to know and be able to do to be successful**. This might have included downloading the app, signing up, putting the app into a folder on your phone or device, or reading the instructions. You'll know you are successful when you know how to access the app and are able to start using it.

After that, you looked for **input**. This is where you learned the content. Maybe you were lucky enough to have someone who **modelled** for you how to use the tool. Maybe you had to look it up, watch a video, read a relevant text, or call someone who knows about the app. However, if the text was too hard, the video seemed too complicated or long, or your friend didn't break down the information in a way you could understand, you had to find another way to access the information. You did that if you were really motivated to learn how to use that app! Otherwise, you abandoned learning and moved on.

Next, you **practiced**. You might have practiced with a friend who already knew the app and received some guided instruction from them. You made mistakes. You got feedback from the task, from yourself, from others around you, and even from your digital device. By that time, you knew what you were trying to achieve, and how close you were to achieving it. When you were not sure of something, you asked a question or sought more information in order to reach the goal. You assessed your progress or showed someone how you were doing and received feedback from them. If you tried something and it worked, it pushed you to try it again in the same way. If it didn't work, you had to come up with something else to try. Finally, you practiced some more, **in different contexts**, with various real-life reasons for making the app meaningful and relevant. You might have practiced independently. You might have practiced in collaboration with a group of friends. The context varied, but you needed to practice in order to determine if you were successful.

Finally, if you liked the app, you used it and **reflected** on the experience. You considered how to incorporate it into your everyday life, and maybe you shared what you learned about it with someone else. It might even have given you the confidence to choose another app to learn!

The Meaningful Lesson Plan

So, let's take what we know about real-life experiences with deep, meaningful learning and move them into the classroom. These six steps can inspire meaningful learning through lesson design:

In school, a student is probably welcomed into learning by a peer or teacher, and/or interest in the subject. Being welcomed into learning is an important way to establish and sustain rapport between teachers and learners.

Preparation breeds confidence

1. Welcome In and Hook: Making a quick individual connection with students before they begin the learning activities. Directing students' attention to a task and sparking curiosity with and for students using the relevant, meaningful, interesting resources and texts available to you and your students.
2. Sharing of Learning Goals and Success Criteria: Co-constructing and sharing learning goals and success criteria that involve students in their own learning.
3. Input and Modelling: Setting up a variety of approaches to teaching and learning so students can discover content and skills to guide their own learning; this is divided into teaching (Input) and showing (Modelling); this process follows the pattern of "I do, you watch" and "I do, you help."
4. Guided and Independent Practice: Structuring and providing a variety of practice opportunities, so students can try, get feedback, and try again flexibly in both collaborative and independent contexts.
5. Checks for Understanding and Ongoing Formative Assessment: Creating many opportunities for both teacher- and peer-feedback throughout a lesson to support learning. Using strategies to integrate assessment as learning and assessment for learning into lessons.
6. Closure: Closing and finishing a lesson by asking students to reflect on their learning and its applications, to think forward. Sparking curiosity for the next lesson.

This lesson design will be based on a 75-minute lesson. It can be modified depending on the teaching situation:

- The time allotted can be modified; however, the relative amounts of time should stay approximately the same.
- If you are teaching a mini-lesson, include the relevant elements, but put more weight on the input/modelling portion or the guided practice portion of the lesson.

GIVE THE LESSON A TITLE

In order to support both teaching and learning, it is important to give the lesson a title and share that title with students. When you stop and consider the title of the lesson, it helps you to focus on the big idea of the lesson and what you are trying to convey, usually in terms of content but also in terms of skills. You can't always spend time being creative but, once in a while, it is a good idea.

SAMPLE LESSON TITLES

Content or Skills	Lesson Title
Fractions	I'll have a big piece of cake, please!
Nutrition	Balanced or not?
Floor hockey skills	She shoots! She scores!

The Lesson Plan for Meaningful Learning is organized to engage your thinking about each lesson you plan and to give you the opportunity to consider a wide range of approaches that inspire meaningful learning. See page 21 for a lesson template that will help you move through the various stages of the lesson, consider different ways of approaching each stage, evaluate options, and focus thinking. Where there are checkboxes (☐), choose the option(s) for the particular lesson. Where there are bullets (·), follow the steps in order to best support student learning.

Lesson Design for Meaningful Learning

Lesson Title: Date(s):   Class:

Welcome In (Establishing Rapport)	Welcome In • Make eye contact • Give a brief greeting • Make a personal connection

Hook (Activating Background Knowledge)
 	
(10 minutes)
	Hook: A short activity that begins quickly and activates prior knowledge, engages student interests and curiosity, focuses attention before the lesson begins.
	
	☐ A quick review of what was learned in the last class
	☐ Ticket in the door or conference on check-in
	    ☐ A review question or prompt
	    ☐ A problem to solve using previous learning
	☐ A video, image, or text displayed with a thinking/guiding question
	☐ An activity to spark student interest/curiosity
	☐ A mindful moment where students breath, visualize, and/or focus attention
	☐ Other: *Write things you will do*

Sharing of Learning Goals and Criteria for Success (5 minutes) *Add standards your using*	• Share learning goals and the purpose for learning to make learning meaningful _____ _____ _____ • Share success criteria (what the students will know and be able to do when they have learned this) _____ _____ _____

Pembroke Publishers © 2018 *Inspiring Meaningful Learning* by Brenda Stein Dzaldov ISBN 978-1-55138-334-7

Input (Teaching) and Modelling (Showing) *I do it while you watch.* *I do it and you help.* (20 minutes)	**Input** Teach and show the content and skills students need to know to be successful ☐ Content Focus: ☐ Skills Focus: ☐ Guiding Question(s) for listening, reading, and learning: _____ _____ _____ _____ **Model** Model examples that clarify understanding and make this learning meaningful ☐ Example #1: _____ ☐ Example #2: _____ ☐ Procedures, task instructions: show/lead the students through hear/see/do steps for success Notes for Accommodations and Differentiation: (☐ content ☐ process ☐ product ☐ learning environment)
Guided and Independent Practice *We do it.* *You do it.* (20 minutes)	Observe, prompt, and possibly meet with a small group of students to support guided or independent practice. Student(s):_____ _____ _____ _____

Pembroke Publishers © 2018 *Inspiring Meaningful Learning* by Brenda Stein Dzaldov ISBN 978-1-55138-334-7

	Content (circle one): Reading Writing Math Science Social Studies Other ☐ Check in on progress ☐ Reteach content and skills ☐ Provide enrichment instruction Instructional Focus:
Checks for Understanding and Ongoing Formative Assessment (10 minutes)	Content knowledge/Skill checks for understanding: Focus on learning goals and success criteria ☐ Observations that focus first on strengths ☐ Conversations that support assessment and promote rapport ☐ Products (for feedback)
Closure (5 minutes)	☐ Lesson review and wrap-up/Reflection ☐ Recording of homework, important information ☐ Closure question/prompt (to spark curiosity for next lesson) ☐ Appreciations

Resources/Materials:

Assessment:
for learning: ☐ observation ☐ anecdotal notes ☐ checklist ☐ conversations/conferencing ☐ work samples/products ☐ check-ins
as learning: ☐ rubric ☐ success criteria ☐ self-reflection ☐ other
of learning: ☐ quiz ☐ test ☐ presentation ☐ assignment ☐ other product

Notes:

Pembroke Publishers © 2018 *Inspiring Meaningful Learning* by Brenda Stein Dzaldov ISBN 978-1-55138-334-7

2

Welcoming Students Into Learning

"If you are interested in something, you will focus on it, and if you focus attention on anything, it is likely that you will become interested in it. Many of the things we find interesting are not so by nature, but because we took the trouble of paying attention to them."

— *Mihaly Csikszentmihalyi,* Finding Flow: The Psychology of Engagement with Everyday Life

The Learning Environment

The classroom environment is crucially important for learning. According to Fraser (2011), the learning environment can even be conceptualized as the "third teacher," after the teacher and students, that can either enhance the kind of learning that optimizes students' potential to respond creatively and meaningfully to future challenges or detract from it. Fraser writes:

> A classroom that is functioning successfully as a third teacher will be responsive to the children's interests, provide opportunities for children to make their thinking visible and then foster further learning and engagement." (Fraser, 2011, p. 67)

Our first step is to refine our vocabulary: instead of thinking about classroom set-up as organizing or decorating, think about it as *designing the learning environment*. This paradigm shift is important. Based on what we know about meaningful learning, well-designed classrooms have

open class design

- Furniture that is arranged to allow conversation and eye contact between teacher and students as well as peer-to-peer; arranged so students and teachers can move easily throughout the classroom
- Spaces for whole-class and small-group work and discussion (input and modelling, guided instruction, independent practice) close to whiteboards, easels, or screens

When you organize your classroom in groups, you are saying both that collaboration and dialogue are important and that there is trust in the classroom.

- Flexible spaces that can be grouped and regrouped in pairs or in small groups for collaboration and dialogue
- Spaces for independent work where students can think quietly, make choices, and guide their own learning
- Places to celebrate student learning
- Places to post important information for students: e.g., agendas, anchor charts, exemplars, learning goals and success criteria, accessible digital and print resources
- Places to provide resources and learning materials for students, organized in a way that allows students easy access

Over my years in schools, I've noticed that classrooms where teachers have rapport with their students are often classrooms where the space is designed very clearly in line with the above suggestions. As well,

- Student learning is celebrated: e.g., bulletin boards with student work displayed, lots of authentic praise for learning.
- Grouped seating (as opposed to rows of desks) is the norm, as students are trusted to work together at times when group work supports learning.
- Resources, materials, and anchor charts are accessible to students.
- Students take ownership of the classroom and move around quite freely without instructions or comments from the teacher.
- The environment is designed and cared for carefully and collaboratively for whole-class, small-group, and independent work.

When rapport is present, often control is shared.

DESIGNING FOR RAPPORT

In a Grade 7/8 split with 36 students, the class ran very smoothly, and the teacher and students were very caring of and respectful to each other. I also noticed that each group of tables for students had a small plant and three mason jars with supplies, on a wooden tray with a pretty placemat underneath. I told the teacher I had never seen supplies displayed that way. She told me that it was important that students knew she cared about them and their learning environment. I thought that was very telling in terms of the rapport she had established with her students.

Welcome In (Establishing Rapport)	Welcome In • Make eye contact • Give a brief greeting • Make a personal connection

Hook (Activating Background Knowledge)
 	
(10 minutes)
	Hook: A short activity that begins quickly and activates prior knowledge, engages student interests and curiosity, focuses attention before the lesson begins.
	
	☐ A quick review of what was learned in the last class
	☐ Ticket-in-the door or conference on check-in
	    ☐ A review question or prompt
	    ☐ A problem to solve using previous learning
	☐ A video, image, or text displayed with a thinking/guiding question
	☐ An activity to spark student interest/curiosity
	☐ A mindful moment where students breathe, visualize, and/or focus attention
	☐ Other:

Welcome Students In

The first area for teachers to focus on at the beginning of the lesson is to welcome students into learning. Of course, rapport is established over time, and daily interactions—in the hallways, during extra-curriculars, and out on the school yard—either encourage or discourage ongoing rapport. There are a number of ways to connect with students at all times during the day.

Making Eye Contact

Did you know that students can often go through a whole day at school without having anyone make eye contact with them or welcome them into learning? They might arrive at school in a group, receive directions to line up as a class, move to the carpet or to their desk to learn, head out for a busy recess, and get started with assigned work. Teachers often circulate around classes during work periods and may stop at individual students, sometimes focused on the work instead of the student.

Think about when you arrive at your own home or to a gathering. If someone is there but doesn't take the time to say hello or greet you, you might feel ignored or uncomfortable. When teachers take the time to establish eye contact and welcome students into learning, students feel as though they belong and that they are cared about.

Giving a Brief Greeting

Each day or lesson, greet your students. Make sure that you appreciate that your students are present, check in with them about big events in their lives (such as a family event, a recreational event, or even a world event if it is remarkable). Ensure that the interaction is genuine and listen for each student's response. When you focus on greeting your students at the beginning of the lesson, you will more likely find a moment to say hello and connect—and, in the process, convey to your students that you notice them and you care about them. If you don't have the opportunity to greet students at the beginning of class, try to do so as the class progresses, during independent-practice time or small-group instruction.

Making a Personal Connection

The tone and volume of our voices conveys a lot to students about our connection to them as individuals. We wouldn't use a booming, "whole-class" voice when greeting a close friend or colleague, so we shouldn't use such a voice to speak directly to a student in the classroom.

It won't be possible to greet every single student before each lesson; however, as students enter the classroom, do the best you can to connect to each student by name as you welcome them into the class. You might choose to authentically comment on something the student has done or said, or something you noticed. Use the voice you would use in a one-on-one, private conversation.

Before you start teaching, you can walk around the classroom and welcome students as you check homework or make sure students have the supplies they need. Simple proximity can be a good way to make a personal connection. How often do you walk around the classroom for any reason other than ensuring students are on task? Proximity is an easy thing to create, and it supports the notion that it's important to connect throughout the day and, when possible, throughout the lesson. Take a moment to look individual students in the eye as you greet them.

In the rush of making sure tasks are completed and students are safe and accountable, we sometimes forget about the importance of tone and the message we are sending with each interaction.

Instead of…	Try…
"Wow! Nice that you finally finished your homework, Steven." (This can be perceived as sarcastic)	"Steven, thank you for completing the homework."
"Jugdip, quiet. We're starting soon."	"Jugdip, I appreciate that you're helping Sarah. You have two minutes to finish up."
Passing by Dorin because she is quiet.	"I love the new haircut, Dorin."
"Mohammed, I hope you'll be paying attention today."	"I checked on that question you had yesterday, Mohammed, and you were right."
"Mahra, please check what you missed yesterday."	"Glad you're feeling better, Mahra. We missed you yesterday."

If we stay aware of our language and approach to students, we can integrate rapport at many points throughout the lesson.

Layer this rapport-building during group or individual conferences with students by looking students in the eye and letting them know you are happy they are learning with you (of course, only if you actually are) or by asking them what they are interested in learning and making an effort to incorporate that into your teaching. Use prompts that include inclusive and caring comments, using the individual student's name to indicate connection:

"Thanks for joining the group, Mitch."

"I remember you had a question from yesterday, Jenny. Was it something about how to complete the task?"

"Para, you mentioned you were interested in how this topic links to what is going on in the provincial election. Let's discuss it for a moment."

"Ravi, we could start with either a graphic organizer or a list. What do you prefer?"

Making students feel welcome and appreciated in the lesson context might take some practice. As time is short, teachers sometimes skip this step, thinking it doesn't fit into their day and into the day of their students. But where teachers find time for it, it makes a big difference in terms of rapport. When students feel connected to their teacher and the classroom community, the results in terms of learning can be remarkable.

Hook

Once students have been recognized and welcomed into your class, it is time to activate background knowledge, engage interest and curiosity, and direct their attention toward learning.

Activating Background Knowledge

Educational psychology teaches us that students need to activate the neural networks in their brains (or schema) to prepare to learn new information.

This part of the lesson is a short activity that begins quickly and activates prior knowledge, engages student interests and curiosity, and focuses attention before the lesson begins. You might refer to this part of the lesson in different ways: minds-on activity; activating schema, background knowledge, or prior knowledge; or tapping into experience. The basic point is that, in order to make sense of new information, learners must connect it with something they already know.

Activities for activating prior knowledge will engage student interest and direct attention. To accomplish this:

- Make sure each student is *involved* to some degree.
- Make students *accountable* to the task, by having them jot down something, talk to a classmate/adult about ideas and being ready to share, get a chance to engage in a discussion with you or a peer.
- Try to ensure that the task is *interesting*; typically, any task that asks students to solve, sort, look for similarities or differences, or share an opinion will direct student attention and spark interest.

Tips for Activating Prior Knowledge
- Do a quick review of what was learned in the last class.

- Prepare a quick ticket-in-the-door: a review of what was learned in the last class using a question or prompt; a problem to solve using previous learning.
- Show a video, image, or text, along with a thinking/guiding question; follow up with a short discussion engaging background knowledge.

Quick Review

By going over what was learned last lesson or class, you frame the upcoming lesson. You can activate prior knowledge by revisiting the last lesson or relevant parts of the last lesson that support upcoming learning. An easy way to do this is to review the learning goals from last class with a simple example or two about what was taught and what is coming up in this lesson that relates to previous learning.

Ticket-in-the-Door

A ticket-in-the-door can also be an opportunity for a teacher/peer conference on a ticket-out-the-door from last class.

A ticket-in-the-door is a short activity given to students as they enter the classroom. It activates background knowledge or engages student interest or curiosity so that students are directed to learning. The ticket-in-the-door can be a math problem, a brain teaser, a true/false, or a which-one-doesn't-belong. It is a quick way for students to see what they remember and do something with the information.

This strategy can help with assessment:

- An assessment-for-learning ticket guides upcoming instruction
- An assessment-as-learning ticket checks student progress in relation to learning goals and success criteria.

It's a good idea to put a title on your ticket-in-the-door, in order to put yet another frame on the learning.

A ticket-in-the-door might be focused on content or procedures from previous learning:

- Include a prompt or question that provides a quick review of some of the relevant content learning from the last class.

SAMPLE TICKET-IN-THE-DOOR: GRADE 2 SCIENCE

Wild Animal or Farm Animal?

Draw a picture of one WILD animal we learned about last class.

Write <u>one difference</u> between a **wild** animal and a **farm** animal.

- Activate previously taught (familiar) steps for completing a task, to make sure students know how to proceed during a given task.

SAMPLE TICKET-IN-THE-DOOR: GRADE 6 MATH

How do we solve an algebra equation?

Question: 4x = 20   **Solve for x.**

Isolate x by dividing by 4. You must do the same on one side and the other.
Divide each side by 4: 4x/4 = 20/4
Do the division: 4s cancel out and you are left with x = 20/4
x=5
Check your answer in the original equation. It works!

Now try on your own:

Question: 5x = 35   **Solve for x.**

For primary grades, you might have to practice tickets with the whole group before having students complete them on their own.

SAMPLE TICKET-IN-THE-DOOR: GRADE 1 PROCEDURES

Getting Ready for Literacy Learning

Name: _____

Draw a line to connect the jumbled statements in the correct order:

First (1st)   Move to station #1 with your group

Second (2nd)   Get out your literacy box.

Third (3rd)   Check the literacy board for your group today.

1 thing I want to learn in literacy today:

- Pose a problem, or give a puzzle or brain teaser that activates prior knowledge, uses learned material, and directs attention.

SAMPLE TICKET-IN-THE-DOOR: GRADE 2 LITERACY

How do we spell it?
Name: _____

Which of these words are spelled INCORRECTLY?

because, thier, night, wich, problim, February

In the next 3 minutes, write out as many of the 6 words as you can, using the correct spelling for all the words.

When you finish, write as many words as you can from the word wall that start with the same first letter as your name.

Show a Video, Image, or Text

This is an easy way to check on content knowledge and activate prior knowledge. You can start a lesson with a video, image, or short text that is connected to the content being taught. These can be funny, thought-provoking, weird, serious—anything that sparks attention. It's a good idea to vary the choice of media so that students won't, for example, come to expect a video at the beginning of each class.

It is important to frame any activity where the students read or view with a thinking or guiding prompt or question, or both. Share these questions using as many modalities as possible (e.g., orally and visually) so students can refer to them. Students need to know where to focus their attention when reading or viewing a text, as it sets them up for discussion or follow up.

SAMPLE TEXTS AND THINKING/GUIDING PROMPTS/QUESTIONS

Topic	Text	Thinking/Guiding Prompts/Questions
Designing Structures (Grade 3+)		Burj Kalifa is 828 m high. The CN tower is 553 m high. What do you think are the similarities and differences, based on their structures? What do you notice?

Anti-Bullying (Grades 3–8)	Video of "You Are Not Alone" at https://www.youtube.com/watch?v=mBwf-VPZqDs	Look carefully at the faces of the bullied children at the beginning of the video. What do you notice? What surprised you as the video progressed?
States of Matter (Grades 4–8)	Show a video on states of matter; e.g., https://www.youtube.com/watch?v=Pu0uZUKSC-s	What are the 3 states of matter? Be prepared to give an example of each.
Environment (Grades 3–8)	• Read aloud Chapter 5 of *Wishtree* by Katherine Applegate • The next day, read aloud Chapter 7. • Use the same prompts both days to activate prior knowledge and direct attention.	What are some actual characteristics of Red, the oak tree? What are some fictional characteristics?

After students listen to, read, or view the text, refer back to the guiding/thinking prompt/question for discussion. In this example, the teacher shares a prompt and then asks a question about a series of images. The teacher also asks the students to tell why they chose their answer and to write their answers on sticky notes. The teacher collects and posts the sticky notes on a chart or board and goes through the responses (which can be anonymous) with the class to look for groupings of correct answers, as well as common misconceptions.

SAMPLE TEXT AND THINKING/GUIDING QUESTIONS: GRADE 2 SCIENCE

Think about the characteristics of amphibians we charted last class.
Which of these are not amphibians and why?
Write your answer on the sticky note on your desk.

This strategy allows you to ask students to respond in a variety of ways. In this example, Grade 7 students are asked to move to a place in the classroom where others with the same understanding or opinion are. Then, students have a chance to talk about their thinking.

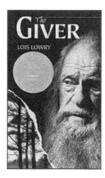

Is *The Giver* by Lois Lowry an example of utopian or dystopian fiction? Think about your reasons for choosing one or the other.

Stand at the back of the class if you think *The Giver* is utopian fiction. Stand at the front of the class if you think *The Giver* is dystopian fiction. Discuss. In 2 minutes, one person from your group will be asked to respond with their reasoning.

Sparking Curiosity

When students are curious about an idea or content, they are more eager to engage in learning. Below is a photo of a Grade 4 classroom door. The teacher changes the Weird But True fact according to what she is teaching that day or week. The students know to expect this. They read the fact, buzz about it, and talk or reflect before the lesson begins. This is a simple and fun way to spark curiosity in your students.

The first five minutes of class can be a great time to create curiosity about the lesson. Sparking curiosity engages students' minds in learning immediately. Typically, it is something rare or novel that sparks curiosity. If you see something unexpected, you look. If you are presented with a challenge, you become interested to solve it. Curiosity is also sparked by one's ability to ask questions about the topic at hand.

To create curiosity, try

- Introducing a challenge into a content area where students have shown interest. Have students try a quick free-write (no rubrics or evaluation) about a topic of choice (choosing from a list of four ideas). For example, if the science class is learning about space and students have shown an interest in the planets, talk for a moment about the fact that there are eight planets in our solar system; share that Pluto used to be a planet but is no longer considered one because it is too small. Show a graphic of the planets in the solar system. Give the students four words: *earth, sun, stars, moon*. Students choose one word and write everything they can about it for three minutes. Then students can choose to share one thing they wrote with a partner or small group.
- Having students observe two similar but slightly different graphics and see what is different about them (e.g., the solar system with nine planets and the solar system with eight planets). Have students think about (and jot down or share on a collaborative digital site) why they think the two graphics are being shown and what they think about them.
- Making it multi-sensory. Try, as much as possible, to involve the five senses in your approach—seeing, listening, touching, tasting, and smelling are ways to keep students interested and engaged as well as curious about a topic
- Letting students generate questions. If you do, students will ask questions that make them excited about finding answers to problems that they are interested in. As well, when they generate the questions, they will stop asking why they are learning what they are learning. If you don't have time to deal with all the questions students have, make sure you put by some problem-solving time during any series of lessons, so students will have the opportunity to research and solve problems relevant to them. Let students wrestle with possible answers before sharing any "right" answers or prepared responses. Students will surprise you as they come up with important information and problem-solving approaches you may not have thought of.
- Providing the opportunity for students to jot down What I Think I Know or What I Want to Know about a particular topic. As early as SK, students can do this (usually in the second half of the year). In this example, SK students have worked on creating a What I Want to Know about living things as a precursor to a research unit about the topic.

Thank you to teachers Ilana Walderman and Amy Rosenberg for this student work sample.

You can use a Reading and Analyzing Nonfiction (RAN) chart (see page 42 for template) to start students on a journey of learning. Students can re-visit the chart on a regular basis to add items or move sticky notes to the various columns as they learn.

Adapted from *Good Choice!* by Tony Stead

SAMPLE RAN CHART: GRADE 3

Name: _____					
Topic: Polar Bears					
Website used: https://seaworld.org/Animal-Info/Animal-InfoBooks/Polar-Bears					
Content	**What I think I know**	**Confirmed**	**Misconceptions**	**New Information**	**Wonderings**
Food	seals, penguins people	✓ ✓		Also eat dead whales	How many people do they kill? Answer: not many; 1–2/year
Appearance	white weigh a lot big paws thick fur	✓ ✓ ✓ ✓		Weigh 330–550 pounds	Why are they white? Answer: To sneak up on prey
Habitat	snow and on ice	✓		On ice and land in 5 nations: US Canada Russia Norway Greenland	

Focusing Attention

Any lesson first requires that you get the attention of the students. If the task is posted and ready, if it includes images or video, students might be curious right away and will attend to the task. Starting with a hook is a great way to get student attention. Remember: *The least successful way to get student attention is to ask for it.* When we wait for students to pay attention before we engage their attention (e.g. "I'm waiting for everyone to pay attention…"), we typically are frustrated and may be losing valuable instructional time. Here are some other ways to direct student's attention:

- Have an agenda on the board with the schedule/activities for the lesson or day; use graphics or comments (e.g., *Art – get ready to get messy*) so kids have an opportunity to get excited about what is to come.
- Put a relevant and/or curious graphic or picture up on the whiteboard with one open-ended question: e.g., *What do you think you see? Why do you think this picture is important today?* Let students think and jot their ideas on sticky notes to be put on a class board or on a digital platform; no names are necessary.
- Start with a quick experiment/demonstration, a problem to solve, or a challenge to consider about the content you are going to teach.
- Pose a question or have students pose a "burning" question they have based on the lesson topic/title. Have them do this individually when they walk into class. Have the prompt on the board as they enter the class: *Write down one burning question you have about _____.* Have the task prepared—paper or sticky notes on desks—so they know how to start.
- Start with a one-minute (or shorter) video and a guiding question for the video based on the content for the lesson; put the video on a loop (or post it on your classroom site) so students can see it more than once to support their thinking.
- Think–Pair–Share: Ask students to stop, discuss, and share their ideas or questions on a topic. This can be done in groups of two or three; with groups of four, it is called a Think–Square–Share. These two minutes can give students the opportunity to express ideas. Circulate during the think–pair–share and prompt or question: *What are you thinking? How did you know that?*
- What Does It Mean?: Start with a word important in the lesson and ask students to define it. You can give the same prompt/word over a few days, as students add ideas to get a working definition of a complex but important word. Don't expect kids to get the "right" answer right away; they can check their own answers during the input portion of the lesson and can co-construct a definition over time.

SAMPLE WHAT DOES IT MEAN?: GRADE 2

> You all have **schema** in your brains that help you learn. What is a *schema*? Write down any single words, phrases, or sentences that you think help explain this word.

Some concepts about schema that might emerge:

- Information in your head that is organized in a way that helps you think about it
- Helps organize both new and familiar information
- Useful because they let us take shortcuts in thinking about the huge amount of information that is available
- Depending on what we already know, schema can cause us to leave out important information to focus only on things that agree with what we already believe or think
- What we already believe or think can be wrong

*SAMPLE WHAT DOES IT MEAN?: **GRADE 7***

You can prove a **theorem** in math. What is a **theorem**? Write down any single words, phrases, or sentences that you think help explain this word.

Some concepts about a theorem that might emerge:

- A theorem is a statement about something true in math.
- Can be proven true by using math
- Part of a larger theory about math
- A *proof* is the way you show a theorem to be correct.
- Example: If two sides of a triangle are equal, then two angles will also be equal; the proof would be a diagram demonstrating this.
- Have you ever heard of Pythagorean Theorem? You can prove it by solving the equation.

Using Mindfulness to Focus Attention

Mindfulness is one way to direct student attention and support the emotional well-being of our students (and ourselves) while building rapport. Research shows that, after eight weeks of mindfulness practice, our brains actually change so that we are able to encourage a relaxation response in ourselves, rather than an angry or aggressive response as a reaction to stress. We can create practices for mindfulness on a daily basis for ourselves and our students to help us consciously control our own automatic *flee, freeze, or fight* reactions in the face of stress. Mindfulness practice helps students (and teachers) focus, de-stress, and react consciously to their own feelings of worry. It is proven to improve psychological hardiness, attention, and adaptation to change.

Mindfulness can be challenging to begin. If you're unsure how to start, here are a few simple ideas:

1. Be open to the power of a disciplined daily practice. To begin, simply pause three times each day to take five deep breaths, focusing on your breath. You can try this with your students too.
2. Enjoy a moment of stillness before the workday begins and set an intention for your work with students, or a particular student, that day.
3. Surround yourself and your students with beauty: plants, rocks, stones, inspiring images, natural materials.
4. Realize that taking time for mindfulness practices in your classroom does not steal time from the business of covering the curriculum; it creates an environment where children feel safe, are more focused, and are more able to learn and participate.

Mindfulness can set the scene for learning, engagement, and attention. Start slow: It can take time for students to get used to this new approach to well-being in the classroom, but they will get used to it and start to see the benefits. Students as young as five years old can easily adapt to simple mindfulness once they know what to expect. Start simply by keeping the lights dim and having quiet/calm music (with no lyrics) on in the background as students enter the classroom; greet them in a quiet voice. The volume and tone of your voice is important in putting students at ease in the classroom and preparing them for mindfulness.

Here are some other suggestions for a mindful moment to start your class:

1. Mindful Breathing

Use a breathing activity as students settle. Have students take their seats and tell them that, in order to prepare them for learning, you are going to guide them through a breathing activity that will calm their minds and bodies. It is important that the teacher breathe along with the students to create a classroom practice for everyone.

Square Breathing

Ask students to sit up nice and tall, making themselves as comfortable as they can. Point out that it's much easier to take deep breaths when our posture is good. Ask students to close their eyes and ground themselves by placing their feet on the floor and their hands comfortably on their laps. Explain that you will try a couple of different breath counts together and then everyone will choose which one feels best for them.

> Inhale for a count of 3
> Pause for a count of 3
> Exhale for a count of 3
> Pause for a count of 3
> Repeat two times

> Inhale for a count of 4
> Pause for a count of 4
> Exhale for a count of 4
> Pause for a count of 4
> Repeat two times

Students can carry on quietly until they are asked open their eyes. At the end, before students open their eyes, ask them to focus their minds on one idea for what they will do to prepare for learning when they open their eyes.

Sunshine Breathing
Ask students to sit comfortably with a straight spine in their seats or at the circle. They should have room on either side to extend their arms without touching their peers. As they inhale, ask them to raise their arms up and out to the side, "like the sun coming up." As they exhale, ask them to lower their arms back down, "like the sun is setting." Do this five times.

Variation: On the exhale, students lower their arms and bring their hands to their chest and belly, "like you're bringing all the warm sunlight into your body."

Five-Finger Breathing
Ask students to sit in a comfortable sitting position. They can rest their hands in their laps and prepare to use one hand to count their breaths. It is important to remind them to breathe at their own relaxed pace and, if they are comfortable, to close their eyes so that this can be an internal experience. Demonstrate for them as they breathe deeply:

> Inhale, exhale, and fold in the thumb in (1)
> Inhale, exhale, and fold in the second finger (2)
> Inhale, exhale, and fold in the third finger (3)
> Inhale, exhale, and fold in the fourth finger (4)
> Inhale, exhale, and fold in the little finger (5)

Finish by asking them to relax their hand and sit in silence until they are asked to open their eyes.

2. Mindful Listening/Visualizing
Based on the topic they are going to study (e.g., weather) or to explore a calming topic or story, ask students to close their eyes and imagine the scene you are describing.

> *Imagine a beautiful, sunny day.*
> *There are cumulus (white, puffy) clouds in the blue sky, and a slight breeze is moving the clouds ever so gently. Think about the sky and how it makes you feel.*

(pause) *Suddenly, and almost without warning, the cumulus clouds turn thin and the blue sky turns a little greyer. A chill can be felt in the breeze. Think about the sky and how it makes you feel.* (pause)

See Dana Chapman's website and blog at www.beebirch.com for more information about integrating mindfulness into the classroom setting.

When students open their eyes, ask them to think to themselves or quietly share their feelings with a peer.

As attention is directed to the hook, and stress is decreased, students feel safe, are interested and curious, and are set up for new and meaningful learning.

RAN Chart

What I Think I Know	Confirmed!	Misconceptions	New Information	Wonderings

Pembroke Publishers © 2018 *Inspiring Meaningful Learning* by Brenda Stein Dzaldov ISBN 978-1-55138-334-7

3

Sharing Learning Goals and Success Criteria

©Glasbergen
glasbergen.com

"Yes, this will be useful to you later in life."

DESIGNING THE SECOND STEP

Sharing of Learning Goals and Criteria for Success (5 minutes)	• Share learning goals and the purpose for learning to make learning meaningful _____ _____ _____ • Share success criteria (what the students will know and be able to do when they have learned this) _____ _____ _____

Learning Goals

Learning goals are brief statements that describe, for students, what they should know, understand, and be able to do by the end of a period of instruction (e.g., a lesson, a cycle of learning, a unit, a course). Learning goals represent a subset or cluster of knowledge and skills that students must master in order to successfully achieve the overall learning expectations.

Learning goals do the following:

- answer the question, "What are we expected to learn?"
- answer the question, "Why are we learning this?"
- make learning clear and transparent
- build a common understanding of learning between all members of the classroom community

- support students to take ownership of their learning and reflect on their own progress toward the learning goals

Sharing learning goals is an iterative process; i.e., it will happen prior to the actual input/modelling portion of the lesson, and again throughout the lesson as students measure their own progress in relation to those learning goals. Sharing the secret of learning goals and success criteria with students is very important in supporting learning and achievement. Having short- and long-term goals, and writing them down, helps with motivation and organization of time and resources. It is also a useful life skill. In fact, many top achievers, including high-level athletes, set goals for themselves every day and strive to reach those goals. As much as athletes have long-term goals (e.g., make it to the playoffs), they also have short-term goals that help them get there (e.g., 30 minutes of cardio and 60 minutes of weight training every day). Setting short-term goals helps people reach the long term-goals that are crucial for success.

When planning, teachers often write out the curriculum expectations to guide their own planning, as well as to build the content knowledge necessary to teach the information. Those expectations are typically written in language targeted to adults; they can be changed into student-friendly learning goals that the students will understand based on the lesson you are planning. The curriculum expectations are detailed in terms of what students are expected to learn. They can be broken down into smaller, short-term goals, depending on where students are in their learning. The short-term goals will be the lesson goals, and the long-term goals might be the unit goals or yearly goals. Therefore, teachers need to work to focus on small steps while making students aware of the larger reason for learning for the unit or year. For example, in a unit about fractions, this is what students need to know:

Purpose for Unit: We are learning to add, subtract, and multiply fractions in order to understand parts of a whole.

Purpose for Lesson: We are learning to create like denominators and add fractions using manipulatives (piece of a circle or piece of a rectangle) and then on paper, in order to help us understand how to add parts of a whole.

Once the purposes for learning have been shared, students can be partners in co-constructing the learning goals, based on their own knowledge and experience. For the purposes above, students must have the opportunity to

- Add to/change/experiment with the "in order to…" part of the purpose, based on their own experiences and understandings
- Add examples to the purpose, in order to allow them to show their understanding about the specifics of what they are learning. Take, for example, the language we use when ordering in a bakery or at a butcher shop. Often, we order in fractions (½ pound, 2 ½ kilograms) and we may need to add fractions to help us make good decisions.
- Support meaning-making or create the environment to help them track their own learning progress in relation to the goal

Learning Goals in the Classroom

On the Grade 3 Math wall shown here, the math learning goal is posted on the anchor chart on the right. It says "Equivalent Fractions: We are learning that equivalent means equal!" The goal is written in simple language for the students, with multiple representations of the meaning of the goal created by both the teachers and the students and posted on the math wall. I like the idea of defining the terms in the learning goal on the anchor chart, to ensure that students understand what they are learning. Your charts don't need to be neat or linear, as long as the information on them supports learning.

SAMPLE LEARNING GOAL: GRADE 3 MATH

This Grade 3 example is missing one crucial component: the *why* of the learning. When students are involved in showing the different strategies for learning, it helps make learning meaningful if they know why they are learning certain things (such as why it's important to know that equal and equivalent mean the same thing when discussing fractions), and even have input into why it might be important.

SAMPLE LEARNING GOAL: GRADE 5 MATH

Thank you to Miriam Toste for these anchor charts from her Grade 5 classroom.

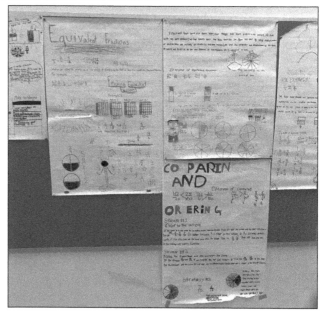

In the example on page 46, the portion that shows student involvement is impressive. Students understand and can list various strategies for equivalent fractions and for comparing and ordering fractions; these charts were built over time. In this class, the students extended the learning through a variety of hands-on projects that supported the demonstration of the *why* of this mathematical knowledge. Often, the problem-solving stage of the unit (where the teacher has students apply their knowledge) gives a hint about why students need to learn what they are learning.

Learning goals have the most impact if

- They are written from the perspective of the student or class ("I am learning to…" or "We are learning to…" or "I can…")
- If they give a reason why (and also leave the opportunity open for students to make their own meaning)
- If they involve subsets of knowledge or skills that are not too large
- If they involve co-construction with students. Once learning goals have been shared, discuss any questions students might have, and come to consensus on the learning goal. As part of the discussion, ask students questions to help them see how this learning connects to the "big ideas" of the lesson or unit.

Much of the time, students have great ideas on applications for what they are learning, and these can make your learning goals even more clear.

Writing Learning Goals

There is no one common template for writing learning goals. For clarity, learning goals are usually written with the following characteristics in mind:

- Start with the phrase "We are learning to…" or "I am learning to…" or "I can…," in order to make it clear that students are learning, and that learning is an important part of the goal.
- Use student-friendly language in the description of the goal. If you need to define terms, do so. Students can't set goals and reach them if they don't understand what they are.
- To support meaning making, add the phrase "In order to…." at the end, so that students can fill in the reason why they are learning these skills or this content.

SAMPLE LEARNING GOALS

Grade/Subject	Less Effective	More Effective
Grade 2/Literacy	We are learning to use stated and implied information in texts to make simple inferences.	We are learning to use clues in the text to know what the author is trying to say (without writing it in words) in order to help us understand the story better.

Grade 8/Arts	We are learning to use the creative process in the arts.	We are learning to re-work a piece of music, dance, or visual art based on feedback from our teacher and peers in order to help us imagine and re-imagine the arts in different ways.
Grade 5/Health and Physical Education	We are learning to read labels on food.	We are learning to make healthier personal eating choices, using information on food labels as a decision-making tool.
Grade 6/Science	We are designing parallel and series circuits as part of our science unit.	We are learning to design and safely build parallel circuits and series circuits, in order to demonstrate how current (or electricity) flows.

Success Criteria

Criteria are the characteristics of a student's product or performance that demonstrate the degree to which the student has achieved the agreed-upon expectations. Success criteria specifically describe, in language meaningful to students, what successful attainment of the learning goal looks like. Success criteria help students understand what to look for during the learning and what it looks like once they have learned it. Quality success criteria make the learning explicit and transparent for students and teachers alike. They identify the significant aspects of student performance that are assessed and/or evaluated in relation to curriculum expectations or learning goals. Success criteria should be simple to understand. If teachers begin with success criteria that are too complicated, students will not be able to relate to what success looks like.

Success criteria

- Let students know what successful learning looks like
- Make the criteria for success explicit for everyone in the classroom community
- Make it possible for students to take ownership of their own progress in learning
- Support common understandings and independence in the classroom

For more on success criteria, see the Edugains website: www.edugains.ca

Success criteria can be presented to students in a variety of ways.

As Statements

Success criteria can be statements about how students will demonstrate what they know and are able to do by the end of the unit/lesson.

As Lists or Checklists

Each statement outlines expectations for success, related to a broader expectation. For example, for the broader expectation of *proofreads and edits own work in a five-paragraph essay*, there would be multiple success criteria, which could be co-constructed with the students over time:

The student successfully met the learning goal if they
- Read own writing aloud to listen for fluency in the writing
- Highlighted main ideas in each paragraph; checked that each main idea is presented in a separate paragraph
- Used transition words to connect the ideas from one paragraph to the next
- Removed unnecessary/extra words
- Checked if writing was unclear or vague, and added details to provide more information
- Checked spelling during a final read-through with a peer

In Relation to Exemplars

Success criteria can be pulled from a good example of a successful demonstration of the learning goal. One way that students come to an understanding of the success criteria for a task is by doing the task or analyzing a product/performance by another student and noting what they did to be successful. Teachers can also use this strategy to identify the criteria:

1. Select a task that involves a skill or a process that students develop over time (e.g., solving a math problem; revising a piece of writing; conducting an investigation).
2. Have students analyze a finished product/performance, or work on a task related to the identified skill or process.
3. When they have finished, ask students to think about what they observe in the successful product/performance or what they did to be successful. Record their ideas.
4. Over a period of time, as students practice the skill or process, add to or revise the list of success criteria.

As Rubrics

Some tasks are inherently subjective, such as an art project or a piece of writing. The Level 3 criteria on a rubric describes the success criteria that are agreed upon by teacher and students and are meaningful to students; therefore, rather than writing out the whole rubric, simply share the Level 3 expectations for success so students will know the criteria. You can include qualifiers like "all of the time" or "most of the time."

Expectation: Write a 5-paragraph essay	Level 3 success criteria
Ideas	<ul><li>My ideas are clear almost all the time.</li><li>I highlighted main ideas in each paragraph.</li><li>I checked that each main idea is presented in a separate paragraph.</li></ul>
Fluency	<ul><li>My writing is fluent when read aloud.</li><li>I read own writing aloud to listen for fluency in the writing.</li></ul>
Transitions	<ul><li>My paragraphs contain transition words almost all the time.</li><li>I ensured transition words to connect the ideas from one paragraph to the next.</li><li>I removed unnecessary/extra words.</li></ul>
Paragraphs	<ul><li>All 3 supporting paragraphs have a main idea and supporting details.</li><li>I wrote proper paragraphs, ensuring writing was clear, and added details to provide more information.</li><li>Each of the 3 body paragraphs has at least 3 supporting details.</li></ul>
Conventions	<ul><li>I made almost no spelling errors.</li><li>I checked spelling during a final read-through with a peer.</li></ul>

Success Criteria in the Classroom

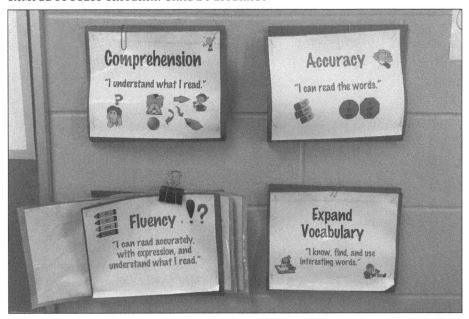

In this example, the success criteria are outlined by the teacher. Each goal (e.g., Accuracy) is the heading, and the success criteria are teacher-created. The teacher added graphics to the posters. It is important that graphics, if used, support understanding, rather than just be decorations on the page. If students help to choose or create graphics, then the visual cue may be more meaningful to students. The fact that the criteria are phrased from the perspective of the student is positive. This would be a great time to get input from the students, especially because by Grade 5 most students are familiar with these terms and have background knowledge and information to share. This example could be made more meaningful by

1. Co-creating success criteria with students
2. Sharing meaningful examples of what success looks like

I showed two of these posters (Comprehension and Accuracy) to a group of Grade 5 students, and they readily shared their success criteria:

Comprehension
- I can make connections (text–self, text–text, text–world).
- I can infer using my own knowledge and information from the author.
- I can visualize the characters and setting to better understand the story.

Accuracy
- I can self-correct (because when I self-correct, it's not an error) to demonstrate accuracy, because that's what good readers do!
- When I make errors, they don't change the meaning of the story (e.g., using "that" instead of "the").
- When I read accurately, it helps me understand the story (so I can check myself).

It is clear that when students have the opportunity to give input or co-construct the success criteria, they have a lot of knowledge about these topics (comprehension, accuracy). Their input makes explicit their own understanding about what they need to know and what they need to do to demonstrate their understanding of the learning goal.

One of the ways to use success criteria most meaningfully with students is to create the success criteria along with them. By directly involving students in the development of criteria, you help them deepen their understanding of what success looks like. The process invites students to share their initial ideas and understandings about the characteristics of successful performance. As learning progresses, you can guide students in exploring and refining their understanding of the criteria by having them continually reflect on and apply the criteria as part of their learning activities.

Students usually have a very clear idea about what they need to do to be successful based on a given learning goal, because most students understand how learning in school works. Sometimes, students give us ideas about what success will look like or will ask questions about unclear success criteria. When you discuss the ideas or respond to the questions, teaching and learning is more meaningful for both you and your students.

SAMPLE OF CO-CREATED SUCCESS CRITERIA: KINDERGARTEN

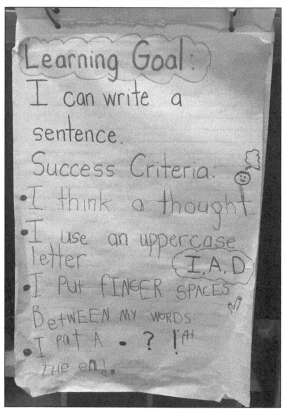

In this excellent example, the teacher started with the learning goal and the first two success criteria. Then the students added to the criteria, over time, in their own writing and with their own visual examples. Keep in mind, if Kindergarten students can do this, it is perfectly reasonable for students in Grades 1 to 8 to be expected to contribute to the creation of success criteria.

Making Success Criteria Meaningful

Allow Room for Personal Experience

There are a number of ways to connect success criteria to students' experiences and make them meaningful for learning. Take this example from Grade 2 Math.

> Learning goal: We are learning to recognize and understand fractions (½, ¼, ⅓) in order to apply the learning to real-world problems like sharing food and understanding money.

> The teacher might share these success criteria (one by one, not all at once):

- I can explain that fractions are smaller than a whole.
- I can show that fractions represent equal-sized pieces of a whole.
- I can use equal-sized pieces of a whole to show if fractions are bigger or smaller than each other or a whole.
- I can explain the difference between a numerator (a part), and a denominator (the whole) because they are very different.
- I can write fractions with the numerator on the top and the denominator on the bottom to represent different fractions, because that's how fractions are written.
- I can figure out how to use fractions to describe simple money problems or how it works when we share food (e.g., pizza).

Students must have the opportunity to question, add to, and discuss the success criteria as they work through a series of lessons. In the class where these success criteria were shared, one student told us that he didn't eat or share pizza, so that didn't work for him. He shared with the class that he eats Daal Chawal and curry with meat, dishes not easily divided into equal parts. Finally, he was able to think of naan bread, which was shared and could be cut into equal pieces. Because he was able to make meaning with that, it was added to the examples within the success criteria.

MAKING SUCCESS CRITERIA MEANINGFUL: SOUP EXAMPLE

Let's return to the soup example. If your friend decided you would be making chicken soup, but didn't know you were vegetarian (because they didn't ask), much time would end up being wasted. Assumptions must be challenged by real experience. So when teaching fractions, the concept could be meaningful to students for other reasons than sharing food or understanding money, but you might not be aware of it. You might choose to teach the "sharing food" problem using pizza as the example. Some kids might eat pizza regularly and share equal pieces of a whole with their family or friends. Other kids may not eat pizza at all, but may instead have to divide a big pot of stew between six people. Given some time, students will think of places in their life and culture where fractions are meaningful.

Give Choice

Another way to make success criteria meaningful to students is by giving them choice on how to achieve them. Take this example from Grade 7:

Learning Goal: We are learning to write 5-paragraph essays using graphic organizers to help organize our thinking, to use evidence to back up our opinions, and to start learning to communicate in a way that is expected in higher grades.

Again, we present the success criteria (not necessarily all at once):

- I can create, identify, and order important ideas and supporting details, and group them into units that could be used to develop a multi-paragraph piece of writing.
- I can create, identify, and order important ideas using a variety of strategies (e.g., making jot notes; grouping according to key words; making charts; drawing webs)
- I can organize my writing using organizational patterns that I have learned (e.g., hook, introduction, supporting paragraphs, conclusions) and use whichever form works for me to accomplish this.

If you are teaching writing and using a graphic organizer, choice can be offered in a simple way: there are some students who prefer a paper graphic organizer, while others prefer a digital one. When learning about characters, there are students who prefer to start with a visual of a character in a narrative, and others who prefer to visualize on their own first. In terms of writing tools, there are students who prefer to use a mechanical pencil and some who like a standard pencil; still others prefer to use a computer from the start of their writing. Any of these are easy choices to give students and have no effect on the outcome of the task.

When working on the success criteria, be flexible about students' approaches to reaching the learning goal or demonstrating the success criteria. In one Grade 7 classroom I observed, the teacher encouraged students to create their own graphic organizers that fit their learning preferences when writing a 5-paragraph essay. In fact, some students preferred not to use one at all. Those students orally shared ideas with a peer or the teacher before writing. Students were given the choice to

- use teacher-created organizers for a five-paragraph essay or create their own
- create organizers digitally or draw organizers with paper and pencil
- use checklists instead of organizers

Two students chose to start writing without an organizer. Since their writing was organized and clear, it was clear they didn't have to use an organizer for writing.

The teacher checked the organizers/methods to make sure that they included all the elements students needed to organize their work, and that students understood the goal and success criteria at all stages. About 90% of the students created their own graphic organizer, which was tweaked from the original the teacher had shared when modelling the task. Many used them online; others liked paper copies. By allowing students to create and use their own graphic organizers, and not expecting students to use the one she had chosen, this teacher was able to make learning meaningful.

Tools like writer's notebooks help define success criteria in this Grade 4 Literacy example:

> Learning goal: We are learning to generate ideas about a potential topic using our writer's notebooks, where we store our reflections, personal stories, and artifacts. We know that sometimes the best ideas for writing come from within ourselves.

In this example, the Grade 4 teacher shared with students that they would be free-writing in their writer's notebooks, as part of the learning goal from the expectation in the language curriculum about developing ideas. The learning goal was posted in the classroom, as well as on Google Classroom for those students using the digital platform.

The idea of the writer's notebook, from educator and author Ralph Fletcher, is that writers need a place to store their best ideas. Each student was given their own notebook and, over a number of weeks, time each day to write thoughts, glue in artifacts, draw, etc. The notebook itself was not graded. After three weeks, the teacher and students co-created these success criteria for writing.

SAMPLE SUCCESS CRITERIA: GRADE 4 WRITER'S NOTEBOOK

Grade 4 Free Writing in our Writer's Notebook

→ We picked an entry that appeals to us

→ We created a title for the entry as the category heading

→ We dated each entry when it is completed

→ We always went back to our work to revise and edit

→ We submitted each entry into our Google Classroom portfolio

→ We always tried to remember, that these entries are honest, expressive, creative and to have fun!

Below the success criteria, a page was provided for students to continue to add additional success criteria over time. The writing that resulted was outstanding, and the students had no trouble developing ideas for their writing.

Making the Learning Meaningful

By leaving space in the conversation to make learning meaningful, teachers can tweak their practices slightly to support students and make a big difference in engagement and achievement.

Often, teachers work to create a list of the learning goals and success criteria for the unit and print/post them on a slide or anchor chart. The list can be hung on the wall or shared during the first lesson of the unit.

SAMPLE LEARNING GOAL AND SUCCESS CRITERIA: GRADE 2 MAKING LISTS

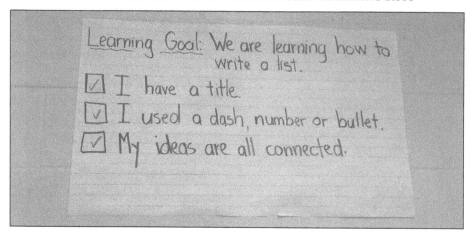

This is a good start. This anchor chart was posted during the first lesson about making lists and then left on the classroom wall to support student learning throughout the year. How can we make this type of anchor chart more meaningful for students?

- Involve students in the creation or monitoring of learning to attain the goals. Leave space on the anchor chart for edits so you can add and delete ideas as students give input into the success criteria and share scenarios for how this is a meaningful or a necessary skill.
- Post at least one real-life reason why students need to make a list, included in the goal or success criteria (e.g., *I make a list in order to keep track of items I want to buy when I go shopping*).

- Try lists with different content, so students see that the skill is generalizable. For example, during writing, make a list of how to get started with ideas.

- Share an example or an exemplar and co-create the success criteria so students can track their own learning towards the goal, using an actual list (as above).
- Invite students to use the success criteria on the chart when list-making comes up in class and continue to co-construct the chart if understandings change. That way, a learned skill or procedure can be integrated meaningfully into future lessons.

When teaching the concept of making lists, this approach works to engage students in their learning in a meaningful way.

It is important to always consider why this learning might be meaningful to students when creating the learning goals or posting the success criteria. If you aren't sure if they understand the real-life purpose, ask the kids. When I asked the students in this classroom when they would make a list, every single student said, "during class" or "on this sheet." Without explicit teaching, the students didn't readily see applications to the real world.

1. Share the learning goal with the students: *We are learning to make lists in order to use lists when we need to make them in our lives.* The idea is to include why this activity is meaningful, why we need to know about this in our lives.
2. Share a read-aloud with the class. In this case, I read the students a picture book, to promote their understanding of when we use lists outside of the classroom. I chose to read *Bunny Cakes* by Rosemary Wells. Another great picture book about lists is *Wallace's Lists* by Barbara Bottner and Gerald Kruglik.
3. Create an opportunity for Guided Discussion and Think–Pair–Share. I posted the guided listening question before the read-aloud: *When do we make lists in our lives?* After the reading, we had a guided discussion based on that prompt. Then students did a one-minute Think–Pair–Share so every student had a chance to share ideas orally.
4. Take the time to brainstorm ideas about how this concept is meaningful to students.

    We came back together to share how the idea was meaningful to them. I spoke to students about when they would use lists in their lives. The students brainstormed a list (a list of lists, as one student pointed out to me!):

- To-do lists (they had seen their parents make them)
- Sticky-note lists (on the computer, using Stickies)
- Hoped-for birthday presents list (before their birthdays)
- A list of things I love about my mom (it can be on any day)
- A list of equipment I need for hockey (before hockey season starts)
- Things to buy to get ready for a religious holiday (so the family will be prepared for celebrations)

5. Add their thoughts about success criteria and the purpose for learning to make lists (the *why*) to the anchor chart. We left space for new ideas that might come up during our lessons about making lists.

In Grade 5, I observed a lesson for which the learning goal was shared orally and in writing:

Today, we will be learning about improper fractions and mixed numbers.

The teacher showed examples of how to convert improper fractions to mixed numbers. About 10 minutes into the lesson, one student put up her hand and asked, "How would this work in the real world? Do you have an example?" Another student raised her hand and said, "What about when I order in a bakery? I know my mom orders 2 ½ pounds of pastries." Another student chimed in, "Or at the butcher. My dad orders 3 ½ pounds of ground beef." The teacher praised the students who had come up with those examples. The student's question about application was reasonable and even expected, as students try to make meaning about what they are learning. Students can help us figure out how to make meaning if we ask them.

Student Choice

When you give students choice about how to demonstrate their own learning wherever possible, you will get a good idea about student learning preferences and how they prefer to make meaning. When students are given simple choice in the classroom, it supports engagement and the continual building of rapport. There are many opportunities to give students choice in the classroom within the context of a shared learning goal and the related success criteria:

The learning goal and success criteria are shared and discussed previously.

- Students can choose how to learn content from video, print texts, or podcasts. You can provide a wide variety of resources, and depending how they prefer to make meaning students can research content with a wide range of options. When students can choose how to learn similar content, and in ways that match their learning preferences, they will be more successful overall.
- Where possible, allow students to choose group work, partner work, or individual work. It is important that students can (at least sometimes) choose who they interact with during learning.
- Students can choose how to show what they have learned. When they are given choice, they become more creative and more engaged. One great way to do this is through a tic-tac-toe board.

3-D Geometric Shapes

Choose your own assignments. You must choose 3 in a a row—across, down, or diagonally—based on your interests and preferences. Mark off the box each time you complete an assignment.

Write a poem about any 3 shapes, describing those shapes in detail.	Choice: Propose a different activity to your teacher.	Reproduce at least 3 shapes using an app.
Write a song about any 3 shapes, describing those shapes in the lyrics. Any style of music is acceptable.	Choice: Propose a different activity to your teacher.	Draw out at least 3 shapes and label them to demonstrate your understanding of those 3 shapes. Use any media you choose.
Go on a nature walk and record your findings about at least 3 shapes you see in the environment.	Choice: Propose a different activity to your teacher.	Create a game to teach us details about at least 3 different shapes.

Once students know the goals of learning and the criteria for success, they are prepared for participation in a wide variety of pedagogies to inspire deep learning.

4

Presenting Input and Modelling

"It is the supreme art of the teacher to awaken joy in creative expression and knowledge."

— *Albert Einstein*

The input and modelling part of the lesson is known as the *teacher-directed* or *explicit instruction* part of the lesson. It is when the teacher, as one of the knowledgeable individuals in the room, directs students to content or skills that are necessary to learn, based on the articulated outcomes from the learning goals. Input and modelling is are both part of explicit instruction, a pedagogical approach that is key to the learning process. Explicit instruction

- Provides structured learning, clear direction, and specific processes for learning. It supports the use of declarative language in teaching, which uses direct language to explain tasks or give instructions; e.g., instead of "Please get started," declarative language would be "Please open your book to page 3 and start reading on the left."
- Requires the teacher to model the use of learning strategies by verbalizing thought processes, including the steps of a learning strategy or process; e.g., "First, I'm going to take all the things out of my literacy box, lay them on the table, and start reading my book."
- Provides opportunities for students to watch, listen, and also participate in practice using a learning strategy.
- Directs students to important information (content) and processes or skills they will need to complete a task; this is best done using as many modes as possible (e.g., audio, visual, etc.).

Input

Input refers to the instruction that you provide to help students access the content to reach the learning goals (*I do, you watch*). You can also provide a guiding question for learning by posting one prior to the input portion of the lesson; e.g., in a lesson on polar bears, the guiding question could be, "What are two new facts you learned about polar bears that you didn't know?" or "Do you think polar bears are important in their habitat?" With a guiding question, students know what to focus on when they become involved in the lesson through prompts and questions. At this point in the lesson, students are watching and taking notes or responding to prompts/questions as you teach content or skills using a wide variety of texts and pedagogical approaches.

Be aware of the level of difficulty of instruction. The level of difficulty should be in the zone of proximal development (Vygotsky, 1978) as much as possible. This means that instruction should not be too hard, which will cause frustration, or too easy, where the student doesn't need instruction at all. When a student is in the zone of proximal development appropriate to this stage, some degree of guidance or instruction is needed from a skilled other (a teacher or more capable peer) to support learning. You'll know approximately where students are in their learning through oral or short written check-ins. If the lesson is too hard or too easy, students will disengage from the material. Err on the side of too easy, but don't teach if students don't possess background knowledge. If you are unsure, check before the lesson through a ticket-in-the door or through a ticket-out-the-door during the preceding lesson.

Although the term *zone of proximal development* is sometimes used synonymously with the term *scaffolding*, in fact they are not the same. Scaffolding consists of the actual activities provided by the teacher or more skilled other to support students through the zone of proximal development. (See also Gradual Release of Responsibility on page 79.)

	Input & Modelling	Guided Practice	Independent Practice
Teacher Support (decreasing)	High/ Moderate teacher support	Low teacher support	Low teacher support
Student Control (increasing)	Little/Low student control	Moderate student control	High student control
Teaching Paradigm	*I do it while you watch/ help.*	*We do it.*	*You do it.*
Difficulty of Learning	Challenging; requires collaboration with a supportive teacher	Just right; within reach with some collaboration with a supportive teacher or peer	Easy; student is able to learn independently

Based on (Pearson and Gallagher, 1983) and Vygotsky (1978)

Teaching Instead of Telling

The input portion of the lesson is the opportunity for the teacher to actually teach. Avoid defaulting into a "telling" mode, merely describing the content to be learned or the steps needed to complete a task, as in this Grade 2 example:

Boys and girls, today we are going to do puzzles that use words connected to the topics we are studying – Spring and flowers. Every time you complete a different puzzle, you will create a different flower. There are tulips, cherry blossoms, geraniums, and one surprise flower. Try to complete two of the four puzzles (at least) today, but more if you finish. You'll have the whole period to work on this and I'll be here to help if you need it!

In this example, the teacher has prepared a task, but the students haven't been taught any content or skills related to flowers, how they relate to Spring, or the steps to complete the puzzles. They haven't been asked to form opinions or been taught how to approach problem-solving when completing a puzzle, or even the *why* of creating flower puzzles. That is why the input and modeling portion of the lesson is so important. This is actually the time to teach a concept, content, or skill, and then model the application of knowledge through examples.

During the input portion of the lesson, follow a set of guidelines for questions when you question the whole class:

1. Get students' attention.
2. Frame the questions, 'Put up your hand if you can tell me…" or "In a moment, I will ask someone to respond…" Try not to ask a question without a question frame, as that will open the door for students to call out.
3. Do not repeat nor rephrase a student's response. Tell the class that you expect them to listen to one another; this will support them in paying attention.
4. After you ask a question, wait for about half the class to put up hands. If you can't get about 50%, then try a Think–Pair–Share or Think–Square–Share to let students process information.
5. Never ask a question of a student you know cannot answer or as a behavior management technique. It's more important to maintain rapport than to put a student on the spot in from of their peers.

Modelling

Modelling refers to the examples that teachers provide to clarify understanding (*I do, you help*). For the modelling part of the lesson, choose one or two examples of the task/activity that consolidates the content and that students will perform in guided or independent learning. For example, you are teaching a lesson on inferring from text, and have shared a read-aloud and think-aloud with students; the guided question for listening is, "Can you think about one time during this reading when you read between the lines to infer meaning from the text?" As the task, students will read a text independently and infer using a graphic organizer. You can model the use of the graphic organizer and the steps to complete it, breaking down the task and the steps and even posting them for future reference. Through modelling, you articulate the specific procedures and task instructions necessary for the students to be successful.

It is important to provide as many and as varied examples as possible; teachers need to be quite knowledgeable in the content in order to meaningfully teach it.

Task Instructions

One of the most frustrating parts for teachers at the end of the input and modelling portion of the lesson is having to explain (and, often, re-explain) the task instructions. Students often do not attend to, or sometimes are unable to understand, this part of the lesson, leaving teachers wondering how to avoid having to keep repeating instructions.

It is important that task instructions are presented in various ways, not just verbally. When the steps are presented verbally only, any students who aren't listening or attending won't know what to do. Some may also be overwhelmed with the amount of information or number of steps.

Here are some ideas to avoid having to repeat task instructions:

- Model the task, then use the modelled task as an exemplar to review the steps to completion. Make the exemplar available for students to review.
- Make sure task instructions are provided both in writing and verbally, and are then made available to students so they can re-hear or re-read the instructions.
- Share the task instructions online (perhaps on your class site) so students can find and refer to them.
- If you feel comfortable onscreen, video the modelling part of the lesson and make the video available so students can re-watch the procedure.

The Importance of Planning

DESIGNING THE THIRD STEP

Input (Teaching) and Modelling (Showing) "I do, you watch" "I do, you help" (20 minutes)	Input Teach and show the content and skills students need to know to be successful ☐ Content Focus: ☐ Skills Focus: ☐ Guiding Question(s) for listening, reading and learning:_____ _____ _____ Model Examples that clarify understanding and make this learning meaningful ☐ Example #1:_____ ☐ Example #2: _____ ☐ Procedures, task instructions; show/lead the students through hear/see/do steps for success Notes for Accommodations and Differentiation: (☐content ☐ process ☐ product ☐ learning environment):

Even though the input and modelling part of the lesson is very important, it should not take longer than about 20 minutes. Your ability to reach your students will depend on planning, for the most part. The length of time will depend on the age and level of engagement of the students. Typically, five- to six-year-olds can pay sustained attention to a task or presentation of information for about 10 to 15 minutes; that number increases with age. We know that the attention span of most students is quite limited, but it can be increased through engaging, well-structured teaching. Therefore, this is likely to be the most detailed part of your lesson plan.

When planning this part of the lesson, take the following into account:

- The importance of your own knowledge of the content, in order to facilitate deep learning and be able to include meaningful examples for the students
- The pedagogies that support student learning
- A clear understanding of the skills necessary for students to demonstrate learning
- The strengths, needs, and learning preferences of each student
- How to present the information in an engaging, memorable way
- How to maintain rapport throughout this portion of the lesson
- Examples that clarify understanding and make learning meaningful

For John Hattie video, see https://www.youtube.com/watch?v=YUooOYbgSUg

WHY NOT JUST SKIP THIS AND GO RIGHT TO INQUIRY/PRACTICE?

In many classrooms, teachers might consider skipping the input and modelling portion of the lesson in favour of inquiry-based learning or independent practice. In fact, skipping the teaching part of the lesson is quite common, but it is clear that achievement is negatively affected when teachers don't actually teach.

John Hattie's work on various strategies in teaching demonstrated that, in order for impact to be significant for student learning, the effect size should be 0.4 or higher. The question, "Why does inquiry-based learning only have an effect size of .31 when it is an approach to learning that seems to engage students and teachers so readily in the process of learning?" is posed to John Hattie. The answer is clear, according to Hattie. Inquiry-based learning works only if a student is learning content, such as vocabulary, ideas, information, and knowledge, and is building understanding. Teachers must teach the content, or there is nothing for students to inquire about. The reason, Hattie says, that inquiry-based learning isn't as effective as expected is that it is introduced far too early in the learning process. First, students need the content and task knowledge before they can work with the content to inquire or problem solve.

Therefore, in order to effect student learning to the best of a teacher's ability, it doesn't make sense to skip the input/modelling portion of the lesson and go straight to the practice or group work, which could result in student frustration and lower achievement.

Examples of Input/Modelling

Lesson Title: Spring Flowers

Input

Content Focus: *Some flowers bloom in Spring, and others in Summer or Fall; we are going to learn about some of the many types of flowers that bloom in Spring. The plants sense the change in weather, temperature, and amount of sunlight when they bloom.*

- *Tulips bloom early, starting in March and usually until May.*
- *Cherry blossoms, first brought to North America from Japan in the early 20th century, bloom in the Spring on cherry trees.*
- *Geraniums are popular indoor and outdoor plants that come in annual, biennial, and perennial varieties, though perennials are most popular for the garden. Depending on the variety, they can bloom in spring, early summer, or fall.*

Skills Focus: *In order to learn as much as we can about the similarities and differences about these "spring flowers" we are going to create puzzles of the flowers to help us look carefully at details, including color, elements of the flower, etc.*

Guiding Question(s) *for listening, reading and learning:*
What similarities and differences do you see between cherry blossoms, tulips, and geraniums?

Model

Example #1: *Complete part of two puzzles for different flowers (morning glory and rose). Show students how to examine the pieces of the puzzle as they build the puzzle and look for similarities and differences. Provide and complete a graphic organizer (Venn diagram) to record findings as an example.*

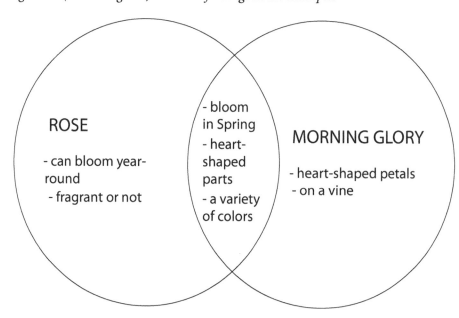

Once the students have received some input, as well as modelling, they are ready to practice the task, perhaps with guided instruction or independently.

Lesson Title: Natural Disasters (Grade 6)

Input

Content Focus: *Natural disasters involve the air, water, earth (land), and weather. They are not under human control and typically cause a great deal of damage to our planet. Let's match the definitions to the terms to understand the main natural disasters that affect living things. When reading these definitions, think about these questions.*

These definitions, videos, and other information can be found on https://nationalgeographic.org or https://kids.nationalgeographic.com

Volcanoes: An opening in Earth's crust that allows molten rock from beneath the crust to reach the surface. This molten rock is called magma when it is beneath the surface and lava when it erupts or flows from a volcano. Along with lava, volcanoes also release gases, ash, and rock. It's a super-hot mix that can be very destructive.

Floods: These occur when water overflows or inundates land that is normally dry. This can happen in a multitude of ways. Most common is when rivers or streams overflow their banks. Excessive rain, a ruptured dam or levee, rapid ice melting in the mountains, or even an unfortunately placed beaver dam can overwhelm a river and send it spreading over the adjacent land. Coastal flooding occurs when a large storm causes the sea to surge inland.

Tsunamis: These are a series of ocean waves that send surges of water, sometimes reaching heights of over 100 feet (30.5 meters) onto land. These walls of water can cause widespread destruction when they crash ashore.

Tornadoes: These are vertical funnels of rapidly spinning air. Their winds may top 250 miles (400 kilometres) an hour and can clear a pathway a mile (1.6 kilometres) wide and 50 miles (80 kilometres) long. Also known as twisters, they are born in thunderstorms and are often accompanied by hail. Giant, persistent thunderstorms called supercells spawn the most destructive tornadoes.

Guiding Question(s) for listening, reading and learning:
What impact do these disasters have on people, structures, and land?
Is there any way for us to stop these natural disasters?
What questions do you have?

Model
Example #1: *Local, Regional, Global*

- *Watch news clips and view a particular Hurricane (e.g., Katrina) on Google Earth.*
- *Together with students, start to brainstorm the impact of a particular natural disaster (e.g., hurricanes) at the three levels: local, regional, and global.*
- *Provide resources for students to view a different natural disaster (e.g., floods) and fill in a similar three-column chart about impact at the three levels.*

For guided and independent practice, have students look at the impact of a particular natural disaster in two different places, and predict which place will experience it worse and why.

See https://www.youtube.com/watch?v=ojiebVw8O0g for a two-minute video on why the flipped classroom makes sense.

Teacher Rachel Albert has created many flipped videos for her work as an art teacher and technology coach. She flips her classroom

- when she does demonstrations
- to catch students up on work they have missed when absent
- to give information
- to share procedures
- to support students who have been absent in catching up

See all of Ms. Albert's flipped classroom videos on her YouTube channel https://www.youtube.com/channel/UCSUVCrhqUhbU4-BHvJeIOIA/feed?view_as=subscriber

Example #2: *Where are hurricanes more likely to strike?*
Examine the differences between Canada and the United States. Then examine the differences between British Columbia and Nova Scotia. Why are hurricanes more/less common in some places? (Canada's water temperatures are too cold to support these storms at their worst. However, we still do get the effects of heavy rain and winds from hurricanes, sometimes with devastating effects).

THE FLIPPED CLASSROOM: A DIGITAL SOLUTION

Trying something new is a great way to support student learning during your lessons. One innovative way to approach input and modelling is the *flipped classroom*. In order to avoid the issue of requiring that students learn the exact same information at the exact same pace during a whole-class lesson, flipping the classroom is a great alternative that supports the wide range of students in your classroom. Students have different needs, and flipping the Input/Modelling step of the lesson allows you to work in small groups or independently with each student during class time, rather than delivering a lesson to the whole class at once.

1. Videotape the lesson/part of the lesson that lends itself to re-watching or reviewing. This can be intimidating, so start with an amateur approach: use your smart phone or tablet to videotape your teaching and post the unedited version for students to watch. Possible starting videos include

   - A demonstration flip when you are showing a science experiment, an art activity, or how to complete a math problem
   - An informational flip when you simply need to lecture or share information with your students
   - A procedural flip when you want to show students the steps for something that you tend to do repetitively, such as lining up, preparing for a fire drill (maybe the Vice-Principal or Principal will participate in this), cleaning up or organizing a particular area in the classroom, getting started with technology, caring for books, etc.
   - An absent flip when you are away from the classroom; rather than leaving the Input/Modelling or instructions for a supply teacher to deliver, simply videotape yourself and arrange for the supply teacher to share the video with your students.

2. It might take you some time to get started, but once you have a little practice and a bank of lessons, you will simply assign the viewing to the students.
3. Students can watch the lessons at school or even at home. Instead of 20 minutes of homework exercises, the homework can be the lesson viewing. Students can pause and rewind if they want to hear or see information again; they can fast forward through the parts they find easy. Students can be encouraged to take notes throughout the lesson they view. Accountability can be made possible by providing the next day a short ticket-in-the-door that involves information from the lesson viewed at home.

4. If you decide to flip your classroom, you can be with different individuals or groups of students during instructional time, moving right to the independent/guided practice portion of the lesson. In the traditional model, the teacher stands between the students and the knowledge. In the flipped model, the teacher acts as a *guide-on-the-side*, helping students access the knowledge at their own pace and use their strengths and effort to spend more time practicing.

Making Input/Modelling Meaningful

By definition, teaching a whole class at one time is challenging. It means engaging the interests, preferences, and background knowledge of 20 to 30 different students at the same time to teach curriculum that may or may not be interesting or relevant to all students. Your task is to draw on students to make the curriculum meaningful and relevant to the best of their ability and to design learning experiences that engage students. Instead of thinking about the curriculum as the driver, think about the group of learners as the driver.

STUDENT-DRIVEN LEARNING: THE SOUP EXAMPLE

Let's say you are teaching students how to make soup (assuming there is a curriculum that would expect students to know how to do this!).

1. Students are made aware that the focus of the lesson is to learn to make soup and understand why we eat soup in so many different cultures. The examples you choose are your best attempt to make this meaningful for all students. However, you realize that not all students have ever tasted, say, chicken noodle soup, so students who have are advantaged by the examples you choose.
2. You ensure that all students can see the instructional space.
3. You introduce a guiding question or two for the lesson: *Think about times when you have prepared or eaten soup. Does this lesson echo your experiences? What can you add in terms of your own cultural knowledge to this discussion about soup as food and a source of nutrition?*
4. You define the terms. The input portion of the lesson is a good place to teach or review vocabulary specific to the learning.
5. You explain why soup is important (e.g., nutritionally, financially, culturally, etc.) so that students understand there is a reason for this learning. Try to give more than one example in your explanation, such as taste, temperature, consistency, seasonality, and cultural preferences.
6. You have all your materials (ingredients, measuring tools, pots) available. Either you show a video about the process and then discuss it with the whole class or in small groups, or you actually demonstrate the process in real time, mapping out the procedure in multiple ways (e.g., numbered steps, orally, visually, on a chart).
7. You show as many examples as you have time for (e.g., clear, chunky, or blended soup).

8. You set up a practice activity that allows students to learn to make soup, and to reflect on why we eat soup in so many cultures and what purposes soup serves. You can follow up with discussion, checks for understanding, and other related activities.

Best pedagogical practices can be seen as *necessary for some, good for all.*

Whole-class teaching is necessary so that all members of the class hear the same messages at some point in the day. It is also important for classroom community-building. Therefore, teachers should lean on best pedagogical practices during whole-class instruction.

Learning preferences are a person's patterns of strengths, needs, and preferences in taking in, processing, and retrieving information. For example, some students prefer to stand or pace as they learn rather than sit; others prefer visual information connected to auditory input (see and hear); some note-take on the computer while others prefer to make point form notes in a notebook. The more you can allow students to learn according to their preferences, the more impactful learning will be.

Environment

Make sure the environment is safe, both emotionally and physically. Make sure there are no hazards, and don't call on students to participate unless they choose to participate; always have a right-to-pass option for students who don't feel comfortable participating in front of the whole class. Other aspects of the environment to consider:

- Is the instruction happening in proximity to charts, easels, and whiteboard or a screen?
- Can all students see the teacher or focal point for instruction?
- Is the instruction meeting the needs of various learners? Is it auditory, visual, and kinesthetic where possible?

Flexibility and Inclusiveness

Use a variety of resources, materials, and inclusive pedagogies that make use of as many senses as possible. Make sure that they are not too difficult, or that they vary in difficulty and approach; e.g., use a variety of groupings within the whole class. Other aspects of inclusiveness to consider:

- Do you provide guiding questions for the lesson that you shared before the lesson and check in with at various points? Guiding questions can address facts, opinions, or procedures. You can provide one fact-based question that requires students to attend to the information; and/or provide one opinion question that requires students to synthesize information to consider their thinking; and/or provide one procedural question that requires students to remember or pay attention to the steps to complete a task.
- Is the information being presented in more than one way (e.g., orally, visually, and kinesthetically)? Can students move or speak at all during the input/modelling part of the lesson?
- Can you intersperse the teaching part of the lesson with reading, writing, discussion, listening, and viewing?

- Can you incorporate different approaches to discussion, such as paired or small-group processing within the whole class?
- Are students aware of the agenda and transitions before you begin teaching?
- Are you aware of, or meeting, the different learning preferences of your students? For example, consider use of technology, space to walk, accessibility of resources, calming music, lighting, etc.

LEARNING AND RAPPORT DURING INPUT/MODELLING

Sometimes it can seem more difficult to demonstrate rapport as you work through the whole-class part of the lesson. When students are learning with the whole class they may feel vulnerable. It's important to check yourself during this part of the lesson and reflect on how students feel, how you are communicating and praising, and how you are creating opportunities for thinking and active participation. Continue rapport-building throughout your lessons by

- Showing care when students need a little
- Having difficult conversations privately and not in front of the class; stop yourself from commenting negatively in front of the class, even if a child is irritating or frustrating you.
- Checking in to make sure communication is clear and making yourself available for clarification
- Handling questions (and answers) with respect
- Using low-key behavior-management strategies, such as cueing or proximity, whenever possible
- Letting students know they can check in with you if they need to, and checking in with them about how they are doing and if they are learning
- Using humor (not sarcasm) whenever possible

Meeting Student Needs

In order to have the best chance to reach your students and promote learning, consider these "good for all" inclusive pedagogical strategies. They allow students to interact with material, see and hear information, and share their thinking through the process. This can be difficult in a whole-class setting, but it is crucial that students have time to process what they are learning.

Let Them Know What's Happening

- Post an agenda and information/warnings about transitions in a visually accessible space that students can check independently as they enter the classroom.
- Keep mentioning the learning goal and, as necessary, revisiting the success criteria, to provide continuity between the goal and the expectations.

Have Them Do More Than Listen

Try activities that involve talk, movement, action, and active processing. For example:

- Instead of asking the whole class a question and waiting for one or two students to come up with the correct answer, prompt the students to Think–Pair–Share: *Turn to the person next to you and share your thinking for 30 seconds. I will ask someone to share when we are done speaking.* Then, circulate and listen to the brief conversations. This will give you a glimpse into student understanding and ideas. During the sharing portion, many more students will be willing to share their ideas once they have had a chance to think things through.
- Instead of having whole-class discussion that engages only a few students, have sticky notes available (either on paper or online); have students put an answer on a sticky note and then get up and put in on a chart in the classroom. The movement, mental break, and opportunity to participate are all important in supporting learning and also help you see more ideas from students.

Help Them Focus

Use guided questions as a focus for the lesson. If you provide some guided questions for listening, students will be more focused on the lesson. Types of questions asked can include both fact-based and higher-level questions. Give small-group–discussion time for them to engage with the guiding questions: "I will give you two minutes to discuss question #1, and then I will ask someone from your group to share back your thinking."

Help Them Engage

- Use technology, small- and large-group discussion, thinking and responding prompts, and demonstration to engage students through novelty and interest.
- Be enthusiastic! If you are excited about the content and demonstration, students will be more interested in the lesson. Give short, personal anecdotes about the learning throughout the lesson; i.e., how you, yourself, made/make meaning with this content.

Keep It Meaningful to Them

- Contextualize the information as you teach. Continually reflect on why the content is relevant and meaningful; ask students for their input on this. Too often, the actual content of the lesson can be boring. So continually make it relevant by referring to the hook, the meaning that was made through the hook, and the stated learning goals.
- Use student ideas. Acknowledge student input and integrate it into the lesson where possible. Where it isn't possible, provide a Parking Lot where students can post ideas and thoughts until you can revisit them with the class at another, more appropriate time. Parking Lots can be provided in print or digitally, or both.

See page 76 for Parking Lot template.

PARKING LOT FOR VISUALIZING WHILE READING
Share your thinking throughout the lesson. Jot any idea down on the a sticky note and "park" it. I will review your thoughts either at the end of the lesson or before tomorrow's class and address your thinking. I promise!

I want to tell you that I see it in color!

Is visualizing the same as making connections?

Do I have to see a movie in my head cause I don't. I see pictures!

Make Accommodations and Differentiation Work for Them All

Accommodations are special teaching and assessment strategies, human supports, and/or individualized equipment required by a student to learn and to demonstrate learning. Differentiated Instruction is a method of teaching that attempts to adapt instruction to suit the differing strengths and needs, interests, learning preferences, and readiness to learn of individual students by addressing content, process, product, and the learning environment.

In an inclusive classroom, *necessary for one, good for all* pedagogical strategies required for some students actually support the learning for all. When planning for and teaching the input/modeled portion of the lesson, it is important to check on the accommodations for all students; all students must receive the opportunity to learn through your differentiation. When you do this, learning is more accessible to all students. Here are some strategies and examples:

SAMPLE INSTRUCTIONAL ACCOMMODATIONS / DIFFERENTIATION STRATEGIES

Instructional Accommodation (necessary for one)	What is accommodated or differentiated?	Differentiation Strategy (good for all)
Note-taking assistance or duplicated notes by a peer; notes are made available for one student	Process	Make notes available on digital slides, a class learning forum, or point-form notes on the interactive whiteboard or chart paper; students can take a photo of class notes/lecture notes if necessary.

Large-size font	Content	Post all readings and notes on a digital forum so that students can change font as necessary and according to their preferences.
• Use graphic organizers to scaffold writing • Chunk instructions	Content and Process	Model how to use graphic organizers and make them available to all students, as needed, prior to writing. Provide a lesson agenda. Make sure all instructions are available, step by step, after (or when) the instructions are given orally to allow students to work independently.
Digital options	Content and process	If possible, make all documents available in both print and digital format. When needed, load documents into a reader app to support decoding as necessary.
Quiet setting; minimize distractions	Environment	Create flexible spaces in your classroom; give students choice about where they sit, when possible. Use a calm and relaxed voice with students.

Allow choice in demonstration of learning	Product	Whenever possible, give your students choice about how to demonstrate success criteria. Choices can include assignments, performances, or a variety of products. Even within a written task, students can be given genre options; e.g., to write a song, poem, or story.

Parking Lot

PARKING LOT

Share your thinking throughout the lesson. Jot any idea down on a sticky note and "park" it. I will review your thoughts either at the end of the lesson or before tomorrow's class and address your thinking. I promise!

Pembroke Publishers © 2018 *Inspiring Meaningful Learning* by Brenda Stein Dzaldov ISBN 978-1-55138-334-7

5

Ensuring Guided and Independent Practice

"Education is not an affair of 'telling' and being told, but an active and constructive process."

— *John Dewey*

DESIGN THE FOURTH STEP

Guided and Independent Practice *We do it.* *You do it.* (20 minutes)	Observe, prompt, and possibly meet with a small group of students to support guided or independent practice. Student(s): _____ _____ _____ _____ Content (circle one): Reading Writing Math Science Social Studies Other ☐ Check-in on progress ☐ Reteach of content and skills ☐ Enrichment instruction Instructional Focus:

When you have finished teaching the Input/Modelling part of the lesson, it is time for students to consolidate their knowledge and practice the content and skills from the lesson. Guided instruction and independent practice occur simultaneously during this longer block of time during the lesson. At any given time, some students will be participating in guided instruction, while others will practice knowledge and skills independently. Independently working students will use available classroom supports, such as anchor charts or posted learning goals/success criteria, the Input/Modelling portion of the lesson, texts or resources available in class, and feedback from peers or, when available, the teacher.

- Guided instruction is typically small-group, paired, or one-on-one instruction facilitated by the teacher for a short period of time. It is meant to develop meaningful understanding of concepts or skills. Guided instruction can occur in any content area, and typically is planned around a specific focus that is informed by assessment information.
- Independent practice is the time when students work independently on content and skills previously taught, without direct support from the teacher or more knowledgeable others.

Based on assessment for learning before and during the lesson, teachers know that typically most students (80%) will be able to practice the content and skills presented in the lesson independently, either alone or in small groups. Some of those students (20% of the class) will benefit from enrichment instruction in which you extend the learning. That means 20% of your students will need some support from you in the form of reteaching an aspect of the lesson to support independence. All students will participate in guided instruction for the purpose of checking in on goals and receiving feedback. Sometimes, teachers think of guided instruction as a way to help only students who struggle, but all students should have some opportunity for guided instruction. The general rule of thumb is as follows for a class of 25 students:

- Check-In on Progress: Fifteen (about 60% of) students will be able to move to independent work after the Input/Modelling part of the lesson. These students will benefit from guided instruction focused on check-ins, opportunities for assessment as learning, goal-setting, and feedback.
- Reteach Content and Skills: Five (about 20% of) students will require intensive guided instruction in order to support their ability to work independently after the Input/Modelling part of the lesson. This type of guided instruction will have an instructional focus; plan to reteach a previously taught concept either in a different way or by allowing a smaller group of students to participate in practice with guidance. These students will benefit from focused instruction, reteaching of content or re-sharing of modelled instruction, opportunities for assessment as learning, goal-setting, and feedback.
- Enrichment Instruction: Five (about 20% of) students will easily move to independent work and require extensions for their learning. This can be in the form of guided instruction that focuses on horizontal enrichment (higher-level thinking, challenges on the topic, interest-based projects or problems). These students will also benefit from opportunities for assessment as learning, goal-setting, and feedback.

If you have chosen to flip the classroom (see page 68), the Input/ Modelling part of the lesson will be shorter and this part of the lesson will be longer; you will have a longer block and more opportunities for guided instruction and time to support independent practice.

Check-In on Progress: gather students with their ideas; restate the learning goal; have students decide if they have generated ideas using the strategies; share ideas generated and share feedback from teacher and peers

Reteach Content and Skills: reteach the lesson; brainstorm various possible ways to generate ideas for writing; create an anchor chart for each student; have students generate one or two ideas to start their thinking.

Enrichment Instruction: extend the ideas generated to more complex topics; start the writing together and discuss how new ideas are generated throughout a writing piece; use a more complex organizer to teach students about secondary ideas in a story.

Guided Instruction

GRADUAL RELEASE OF RESPONSIBILITY

The Guided/Independent Practice part of the lesson is based on the gradual release of responsibility model for optimal learning. In this model, guided and independent practice require that the learner have a good deal of control over the learning; the teacher still supports the learning, but to a lesser degree than in the Input/Modelling portion of the lesson. This relates to the zone of proximal development discussed on page 62.

This model reflects the level of challenge, with Guided Practice being in the students' zone of proximal development; see page 62.

	Input & Modelling	Guided Practice	Independent Practice
Teacher Support (decreasing)	High/ Moderate teacher support	Low teacher support	Low teacher support
Student Control (increasing)	Little/Low student control	Moderate student control	High student control
Teaching Paradigm	*I do it while you watch/ help.*	*We do it.*	*You do it.*
Difficulty of Learning	Challenging; requires collaboration with a supportive teacher	Just right; within reach with some collaboration with a supportive teacher or peer	Easy; student is able to learn independently

Based on (Pearson and Gallagher, 1983) and Vygotsky (1978)

This model helps show the level of support needed in the various areas of the lesson. We see that the Guided and Independent Practice steps are the part of the lesson where students are mostly or fully independent. If the work is truly independent, then you are freed up to work with a different small group of students who require guided practice.

For guided practice, take a small group (two to five students) with similar needs to

- Create a space to have a dialogue with the group about the topic being studied
- Reteach the content or process for successful learning
- Allow students to practice independently (with supervision) and ask questions as necessary, based on an instructional focus
- Support the learning by questioning, dialogue, prompting, and feedback

In order for guided instruction to be successful, this part of the lesson

- happens in a small-group setting; e.g., at a small table or space where the students are gathered
- is active on the part of both the teacher and students
- is based on previous assessments of student learning/assessment as learning, which can take the form of observations, conversations, or products, and requires learning goals and success criteria
- is differentiated according to the needs to the students: content, process, product, and learning environment
- is structured and planned for guided, and then independent, practice
- is where students feel safe and supported to attempt something that is a little challenging (rapport is important for this to be successful)

This part of the lesson is *an opportunity*. Teachers are always searching for time to work with students in small groups or provide one-on-one attention to support student learning (either with students who are struggling or those who are handling the work easily), and this part of the lesson provides the space to do so. Teachers must avoid perceiving guided instruction time as

- a chance to sit at their desk waiting for a student to "need help"
- a cheerleading session, where they walk around saying "Good for you," "Keep it up," "Keep going."
- a time to help one student at a time as they struggle with work that is meant to be independent

From Guided Reading to Guided Instruction

When teachers think of guided instruction, they often think of *guided reading*. Many teachers are familiar with guided reading as the time during the literacy block when the teacher chooses a small group of students and reads with them, using a text at the appropriate instructional level (determined through assessment) and with a focus for instruction. The guided reading lesson plan is a framework for guided reading, on which the teacher can check off, fill in, and circle relevant teaching points for any given lesson.

Note that this process mirrors the work done in guided reading. There is a brief *before* part where the purpose, focus, goals are articulated clearly, that includes dialogue or discussion/ feedback and debugging of task or unfamiliar content; a *during* part, where the students practice, and the teacher supervises, listens in, prompts, and praises, giving meaningful feedback; and, finally, an *after* part, or wrap-up, setting up students to work independently moving forward.

Text: Level: Author:	Genre (circle one): Fiction Non-Fiction Poetry/Prose

SETTING THE STAGE: BEFORE READING (5 minutes)
(Explicit strategy instruction)
Strategy instruction linked to chosen text and learning goal:
- Orientation to the new book/text introduction/activating prior knowledge/making connections
- Point out new vocabulary/unusual language structures
- 2–3 new words from the text to solve/word work:

_____

- Whiteboard/magnetic letters/digital approach to work on spelling or show the student a word in another context
- Share during and after reading goals (can be co-constructed)

Instruction or Assessment Notes:

DURING READING: PRACTICE (10 minutes)
(Students read either quietly or silently and the teacher listens in, prompts, and praises)
- Let the student read part of the text independently
- Praise the student for use of strategies/meaningful attempts at solving
- Prompt the student for visual cues: *Does it look right? Get your mouth ready for the first letter. Look for a part in the word that you know.*
- Prompt the student for meaning cues: *Does it make sense? Check the picture.*
- Prompt the student for structure: *Does it sound right? Can we say it that way?*

Instruction or Assessment Notes:

AFTER READING: DISCUSSION AND REFLECTION (5 minutes)
(Responding to reading)
- Descriptive feedback: individually or to the group
- Praise point: based on what you noticed during the reading
- Teaching point: connected to praise point, if possible
- Comprehension dialogue: teacher and students discuss the story
- Follow-up responses: points of view, connections, details, summarize, key concepts, draw conclusions, share insights and understandings

Assessment Notes:

Guided reading is, like guided instruction, a small-group structure that includes whatever types of goal-setting, strategy instruction, discussion, feedback, support, and practice students need in order to progress in their learning. This should typically take a short teaching time before the guided practice, usually for students to practice a skill or consolidate content, and a quick closure to discuss the learning that has occurred.

As familiar with guided reading as many teachers are, it is important to understand that guided instruction can occur in any subject area. The basics of guided instruction are the following:

- a small group of students
- an instructional focus determined through previous or current assessment for/as learning
- an introduction, action, and follow-up
- the goal of students being mostly independent during guided instruction
- the teacher's presence to support learning

Here is an example of guided instruction in the area of nonfiction writing.

In the Input/Modelling portion of a lesson on informational writing, the teacher:
- Bases the topic on student interests as much as possible in the area of nonfiction writing
- Shows students a graphic organizer and models how to work with it to write an informational paragraph
- Teaches students how to research a topic; e.g., using Internet bookmarks, using relevant digital or print texts
- Hears from some students who share their thinking and questions during the whole-class lesson; possibly adds to or edits success criteria for the task
- Provides each student (on paper or digitally) with a copy of the graphic organizer and allows them to begin with the first section.

SAMPLE INFORMATIONAL WRITING GRAPHIC ORGANIZER

Topic or Area of Interest	
Research Findings and New Vocabulary	
Topic Sentence	
Three important details	1. 2. 3.
Conclusion	

First Draft of Paragraph	

As noted previously, following the Input/Modelling portion of the lesson, the whole-class lesson will not equip all students to start writing independently. Many students will still need some support with topic, research, and vocabulary, or paragraph structure. This is where guided instruction comes in.

Planning for Guided Instruction

This step of the lesson always requires a "plan within a plan." First, ensure that students who are not receiving guided instruction are able to work independently if they are given supports that do not involve the teacher for about 20 minutes. Supports include

- posted learning goals and success criteria for the task
- an exemplar of any tools, such as a graphic organizer, filled in for student reference, introduced in the Input/Modelling step
- steps or procedures for the task made available to students
- the assignment of partners or small groups
- access to a video (probably teacher-made) that allows students to re-watch procedures or learn about content in a different way (see Flipped Classroom on page 68)
- a careful choice of tasks: either a problem or a project for students to solve

SAMPLE PLAN FOR GUIDED WRITING INSTRUCTION: GRADES K-8

Content: Focus: Students: (usually 2–5)
BEFORE: SETTING THE STAGE (5–10 minutes) (Explicit strategy instruction) Restate learning goal and success criteria. Engage students in a brief, shared learning experience. Read or tell a short story to support student understanding of an informational paragraph. Engage students in a dialogue or conversation through prompts: • "Tell me more about that" • "How did you know?" • "I wonder if…" • "I heard you say…. Can you explain?" • "I agree with you because…" • "I disagree with you because…"

Have students orally rehearse what they plan to write
- with the teacher
- in student pairs

Explicit Instruction
- Teach one or two specific strategies for writing.
- Teach strategies for one of the traits of writing, including ideas, organization, text and sentence structures, fluency, conventions.
- Provide brief examples of strategies to support students' immediate use. Record examples (digitally, on paper, or on cue cards) as you present them, so students can refer to them later.
- Reflect with students about how they will integrate these strategies into their own writing during the lesson.
Instruction and Assessment Notes:

DURING: PRACTICE (10 minutes)
(Students write either quietly or silently; the teacher looks in, prompts, and praises)
- Provide students with time to write at the small-group table, but individually and as independently as possible.
- Provide immediate individual guidance and feedback while students write
  - Assist individual students based on goals
  - Monitor students while they write and prompt to guide their thinking
- Include a brief sharing activity in which each writer's immediate work is shared with an audience. This sharing will allow each writer to experience their newly written text as a whole.
- Allow students to write independently following guided instruction.
Instruction and Assessment Notes:

AFTER: DISCUSSION AND REFLECTION
(Responding to writing)
- Descriptive Feedback
- Praise point: based on what you noticed
- Teaching point: connected to praise point, if possible
- Dialogue: let students discuss the writing; not all teacher questioning/ student responding
- Follow-up responses: e.g., points of view, connections, details, summarize, key concepts, draw conclusions, share insights and understandings
Assessment Notes:

This same format can be used for any content area and with any text; a video, image, or audio clip (podcast) may also be used as text. The format will stay basically the same, but some of the content will change.

In this guided science lesson, the teacher conducts a short experiment/ demonstration on the density of liquids.

Content:

Focus:

Students: (usually 2–5)

BEFORE: SETTING THE STAGE (5–10 minutes)

(Explicit strategy instruction)

Restate learning goal and success criteria. Engage students in a brief, shared experience. Share a text (audio, video, digital, print) to support student understanding of the concept or procedure you are guiding.

Engage students in a dialogue or conversation through prompts:
- "Tell me more about that"
- "How did you know?"
- "I wonder if…"
- "I heard you say…. Can you explain?"
- "I agree with you because…"
- "I disagree with you because…"

Explicit Instruction
- Teach one or two specific strategies for understanding the experiment; e.g., observation, theory–practice).
- Provide an example to support students' immediate understanding. Record examples (digitally, on paper, or on cue cards) as you present them, so students can refer to them later.
- Reflect with students on how they will integrate these strategies into their own experiments during independent practice time.

Procedure
- Set up beakers with different liquids inside: e.g., vegetable oil, dish soap, water, alcohol, milk, corn syrup.
- With students, label the beakers.
- Make predictions about which will be denser and what students can expect to observe.
- Mix two of the liquids and observe the results, talking the students through the observations and recording them.

Instruction and Assessment Notes:

DURING: PRACTICE (10 minutes)

(Students work either quietly or silently; the teacher looks in, prompts, and praises)
- Provide students with time to practice as independently as possible.
  - Provide immediate individual guidance and feedback while students work.
  - Assist individual students based on goals.
  - Monitor students while they work and prompt to guide their thinking.

- Include a brief sharing activity in which each student's immediate work is shared with an audience. This sharing will allow each student to share their new learning in a comfortable setting.

Instruction and Assessment Notes:

AFTER: DISCUSSION AND REFLECTION
(Responding)
- Descriptive feedback
- Praise point: based on what you noticed
- Teaching point: connected to praise point, if possible
- Dialogue: let students discuss their findings; not all teacher questioning/ student responding
- Follow-up responses: e.g., points of view, connections, details, summarize, key concepts, draw conclusions, share insights and understandings

Assessment Notes:

PLAN FOR ENRICHMENT: GRADES K-8

This guided instruction lesson plan is for enrichment. In this example, the enrichment is provided on the topic of Comprehension Strategies in Reading.

Content:
Focus:
Students: (usually 2–5)

BEFORE: SETTING THE STAGE (5–10 minutes)
(Explicit strategy instruction)
Restate learning goal and success criteria. Engage students in a brief, shared experience. Share a text (audio, video, digital, print) to support student understanding of the concept or procedure you are guiding.

Engage students in a dialogue or conversation through prompts:
- "Tell me more about that"
- "How did you know?"
- "I wonder if…."
- "I heard you say…. Can you explain?"
- "I agree with you because…"
- "I disagree with you because…"

Explicit Instruction (using enriched content, process, product):
- Teach one or two specific strategies for comprehension; in this case, advanced strategies such as synthesizing ideas or using fix-up strategies.
- Have students search for and provide an example to support immediate understanding. Record examples (digitally, on paper, or on cue cards) as students present them, so students can refer to them later.
- Reflect with students on how they will integrate these strategies into their own text reading during independent practice time.

Instruction and Assessment Notes:

DURING: PRACTICE (10 minutes)
(Students read either quietly or silently; the teacher listens in, prompts, and praises)
- Provide students with time to practice, as independently as possible, using a complex text chosen by the teacher or one that that the students choose individually.
  - Provide immediate individual guidance and *feedback* while students work
  - Assist individual students based on goals
  - Monitor students while they work and prompt to guide their thinking
- Include a brief sharing activity in which each student's immediate work is shared with an audience. This sharing will allow each student to share their new learning in a comfortable setting.

Instruction and Assessment Notes:

AFTER: DISCUSSION AND REFLECTION
(Responding to reading)
- Descriptive feedback
- Praise point: based on what you noticed
- Teaching point: connected to praise point, if possible
- Dialogue: let students discuss their findings; not all teacher questioning/ student responding
- Follow-up responses: e.g., points of view, connections, details, summarize, key concepts, draw conclusions, share insights and understandings

Assessment Notes:

With these sample plans in mind, guided instruction is easy to organize, with about 20 minutes set aside to work with small groups of students. In order to make space for this in the schedule:

- Start the rest of the class on an easier task that is truly independent.
- Have students share their learning with each other and give each other feedback, based on learning goals and success criteria.
- Meet with students who require additional challenge, check-ins, or support with content and skills.

Other Approaches to Guided Instruction

There are four other common classroom strategies that can support student learning during the guided part of the lesson:

- Cooperative learning
- Project-based learning
- Problem-based learning
- Flipped Learning

Cooperative Learning

In this structure, students work in cooperative groups (usually created by the teacher with a purpose in mind) according to the emotional needs and learning preferences of the students. The groups are composed of students with different abilities and talents, enabling participants to work together to achieve a goal. Usually, roles are assigned to increase accountability and ensure participation in the group. Students are assigned a particular task and they must cooperate in order to complete the task, looking to one another as supports for learning. Tasks are structured so that no single team member can complete them on their own. During a cooperative learning task, the teacher can guide instruction through check-ins.

Following observation of the group, the teacher picks a praise point and teaching point for the guided instruction (it's best if they are related). Then the teacher facilitates a discussion about the goals, strategies, and instruction required for the group to be successful. Guided instruction would be a task for assessment as learning (group members assess their progress toward a goal and what else they need to be successful) and the teacher guides them toward their goals through explicit instruction and feedback. Sometimes the guided instruction might focus on social skills in the group situation, as this can be a challenge in cooperative group learning.

Project-Based Learning

In project-based learning, the teacher facilitates and structures learning through a variety of different projects focused on a particular topic or theme, allowing students to work on topics of interest to them, at their own level or pace, and in a holistic manner. Project-based learning is guided by goals and success criteria, but these might change frequently, depending on the progress of the group in particular directions. This type of learning can occur in small groups, in pairs, or independently, as suits students' learning preferences or social needs. The teacher monitors the level of the task and gives guided instruction as needed, for content or process, mostly in the form of discussions and ideas for consideration.

Problem-Based Learning

This type of learning allows students to solve realistic problems by reflecting on best strategies and prior knowledge of effective approaches, according to their abilities and readiness to learn. Problem-based learning can happen independently, in pairs, or in groups. The teacher plans these challenges carefully, along with students, to meet the strengths and needs of each student. The teacher monitors the level of the task and gives guided instruction as needed, for content or process, mostly in the form of discussions and ideas for consideration.

Flipped Learning

See page 68 for more on flipped learning.

In a flipped-learning scenario, the traditional learning environment is reversed, often with instructional content being delivered online through a video to support the Input/Modelled portion of the lesson. Students view the video outside of the classroom, prior to the lesson. This creates a situation in which students come to school with the Input/Modelling portion already viewed, giving them more time for Guided/Independent work. Students can re-view the video as necessary and participate in guided and independent work that is traditionally completed at home. The best part of flipped learning is that it allows students to watch the Input/Modelling portion of the lesson at their own pace, and have more time for guided instruction and independent practice, during which the teacher can meet with small groups of students to focus on strengths, needs, and instructional strategies that support further learning.

Independent Practice

True independent practice is wonderful. This is the time when students can complete a task in class without a great deal of teacher support. Teachers will know if a task is independent (*student does; teacher watches*) only when assessment informs the learning and student and teacher both know that the task is do-able by the student alone. In reading instruction, independence is assumed when reading accuracy is 95–100% on a given text, meaning students can do almost the whole task accurately by themselves. The same should be true of any independent task. Usually, students can decide when a task is independent, but some strategies can support students to get to independence. These include

- Using posted information, such as referring to goals and success criteria or exemplars, to guide independent work.
- Checking step-by-step procedures, provided by the teacher or co-constructed by teacher and students together during the Input/Modelling portion of the lesson, before asking for help.
- Learning to ask peers for specific support; e.g., not "What do I have to do?" but "I've started #1. What is the next step?"
- Using group work productively to support independence.

Assessment As Learning

By participating in assessment-as-learning activities independently, students check in on their own learning as necessary. Teachers begin by providing and modelling opportunities for students to assess themselves. Students need to know the learning goals and success criteria, and understand what they need to do to demonstrate those criteria (through feedback). Using peer or teacher feedback, students can assess their own progress through a checklist, referring to a rubric, a ticket-out-the-door, etc.

Here is a sample of an assessment-as-learning approach from teacher Debra Fabian. She creates unit outlines prior to each unit, and this gives students ongoing opportunities for assessment as learning.

SAMPLE ECOLOGY UNIT PLAN AND LESSON LEARNING GOALS: GRADE 7 SCIENCE

Name: _____
Date: _____
Class: _____

Section	Learning Goals	Success Criteria	Self-reflection
1	• I am learning to explain what an ecosystem is and how different ecosystems have specialized needs. • I am learning to understand the difference between abiotic and biotic elements.	I CAN • recognize the importance and relevance of studying ecology • define what an ecosystem is • identify different types of ecosystems, including land, desert, and aquatic ecosystems • identify abiotic and biotic elements in an ecosystem • identify and explain the five needs of a biotic element to survive Other: Teacher Signature: _____ Student Signature: _____	Check ☐ I fully understand what I need to know and be able to do for these lessons. ☐ I do not understand some of the success criteria, specifically: ☐ In order to support my learning, I will:

Each unit begins like this, and the students use the self-reflections regularly. Students also have the opportunity to add to the success criteria as necessary and when agreed upon between teacher and student. When students are aware of the learning goals and success criteria, they can assess their own understanding of progress regularly.

What Can Students Typically Do Independently?

It is important to know what students can do independently so that you can start to plan meaningful yet easily completed independent-practice activities. I have asked many teachers, "What can your students do independently, almost every time?" and received ready responses. The answers were varied but very reliable over time.

Kindergarten/Grade 1

- Write a journal (once it has been modelled a few times)
- Draw pictures
- Complete familiar simple puzzles
- Read to/with a friend
- Work on technology that has been previously taught but has immediate feedback within the program
- Eat
- Watch a video and respond to a simple question
- Do mindfulness activities; e.g., deep breathing, coloring, listening to quiet music

Grades 2–5

- Write a journal or free-write (once it has been modelled a few times)
- Complete familiar practice questions in math, literacy, science, and most other subjects
- Draw pictures to represent their thinking or tell a story
- Complete familiar simple puzzles, based on content they are learning
- Do Google searches (with some framing about critical literacy)
- Use a familiar graphic organizer that has been used before successfully
- Read to/with a friend
- Read alone (if the reading level is easy)
- Word work (if answers are provided for self-checking)
- Work on technology that has been previously taught but has immediate feedback within the program
- Eat
- Watch a video and respond to a simple question
- Listen to a podcast of interest and respond to simple questions
- Work in a group (if the group is well-constructed and roles are clear)
- Do mindfulness activities; e.g., deep breathing, coloring, listening to quiet music

Grades 7–8

- Complete familiar practice questions in math, literacy, science, and most other subjects
- Write a journal or free-write (if they have ideas)
- Draw pictures to represent their thinking
- Do brain-teasers, solve interesting problems, or do puzzles, by themselves or in a group
- Do Google searches (with some critical thinking questions)
- Use a familiar graphic organizer that has been used before successfully
- Read to/with a friend
- Work on technology that has been previously taught but has immediate feedback within the program
- Eat
- Watch a video and respond to questions
- Listen to a podcast of interest and respond to questions
- Work in a group (if the group is well-constructed and roles are clear)
- Do mindfulness activities; e.g., deep breathing, coloring, listening to quiet music

It is obvious that most independent activities are common among all learners, as long as they are mostly familiar, have an opportunity for some feedback, and are accompanied by instructions that are simple and clear.

SUPPORTS FOR INDEPENDENT PRACTICE

You can encourage independence by providing supports, including
- exemplars around the room that may include definitions of terms
- anchor charts (best if co-constructed with students)
- simple task directions, or multiple examples displayed

Here is a sample from Grade 8 class where many exemplars are displayed.

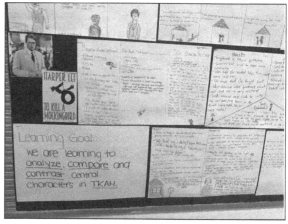

In this example, students use the exemplars posted and compare their own work to them. In this situation, the learning goal is posted and success criteria are also known. Then students can assess their own work again exemplars that were previously shared in class.

Here is a sample anchor chart from a Grade 5 class. The task directions are clear and simple. It even includes one example.

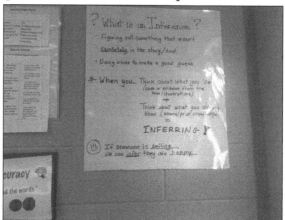

It takes time to build the expectations and structures for guided and true independent practice in the class, but once it is established, it is truly worth it as students have opportunities to practice, based on their abilities and with a little support as needed.

6

Checking for Understanding

*"When the cook tastes the soup, that's formative;
when the guests taste the soup, that's summative."*

— *Robert Stake*

DESIGNING THE FIFTH STEP

Checks for Understanding and Ongoing Formative Assessment (10 minutes)	Content knowledge/Skill checks for understanding: Focus on learning goals and success criteria ☐ Observations that focus first on strengths ☐ Conversations that support assessment and promote rapport ☐ Products (for feedback)

This part of the lesson can happen after guided or independent practice, but the observations and conversations that happen during the lesson are part of the ongoing assessment a teacher does throughout the whole lesson. It's natural to observe, converse, and look at student progress and products; the shift is looking at each of these opportunities as a check for understanding, rather than as an evaluation of learning.

> **CHECKS FOR UNDERSTANDING: SOUP EXAMPLE**
>
> The soup analogy works well here because, just as in Chapter 2, when we looked at having goals and knowing what success will look like when trying out a new recipe, checks for understanding occur prior to the completion of the recipe. It's the time when the chef, who may be teacher, student, or peer—someone who supports the learning—checks in and tastes the soup to see if it is everything that was planned. The chef checks for taste, consistency, and appeal while there is still time to make changes before the soup is served.

Formative Assessment and Checks for Understanding

At this point of the lesson, approaches to assessment are meant to create opportunities to support meaningful student learning, to help students to reach their goals for learning. This is also known as *formative assessment*, which comprises a wide variety of methods teachers use to conduct in-process evaluations of student knowledge and understanding, learning strengths and needs, and academic progress during a lesson.

Anyone who has ever watched an excellent sports coach or coached a team knows that these check-ins are ongoing and that assessment, feedback, and adjustment are key to improved performance. If a basketball player is on the court during practice, that player will have constant feedback and receive suggestions for improvement for that practice period so that, when the game is played, that player will have received all the feedback needed to ensure their best performance. Rather than thinking about assessment as a way of evaluating student learning, see it instead as an opportunity to continually look at progress.

Checks for understanding are a type of formative assessment that monitors student understanding so that teacher and student are aware of student strengths, needs, and progress. It gives students the opportunity to reflect on what they need to do to be successful. Meanwhile, through observations, conversations, and products—basic ways to check for understanding—teachers can improve the effectiveness of their instruction by questioning, explaining, or reteaching as necessary. With formative assessment information, teachers can monitor and adjust upcoming lessons, guided instruction, or independent practice opportunities according to the degree to which students are achieving the desired content and skill outcomes. Therefore, checks for understanding need to go beyond general prompts to include meaningful and well-structured check-ins that are actually assessment opportunities that support learning.

The most challenging part of assessment is knowing the answer to the question "…compared to what?" Teachers must make quick assessment decisions and give feedback to support learning. Experienced teachers know what they are looking for as students practice knowledge and skills, partly because they know what criteria inform learning. How can all teachers feel comfortable in their ability to assess student learning "on the run"? Just as in the soup example, sometimes there is subjectivity in assessment. Some people will add salt or pepper to a soup that tastes great to another. Some people like spicy soup; others don't. In order to control for all of this variability, the best practice for teachers is to

- Understand and share exemplars of student work that demonstrates the learning you are assessing for
- Use moderated marking to create criteria and exemplars. Get together with colleagues to practice giving feedback based on observations, conversations, and products, to get closer to understanding how the criteria look in practice.
- Use co-constructed rubrics and success criteria with colleagues before attempting to do so with students
- Share and reflect on criteria with students on an ongoing basis
- Include student choice, voice, reasons, and opinions in the process of assessment

Assessment that Supports Learning

According to *Growing Success* (Ontario Ministry of Education, 2010), "the primary purpose of assessment is to improve student learning." This is truly the case with the formative assessment that encompasses checks for understanding. This Ontario curriculum document on assessment and evaluation outlines the following as fundamental principles of assessment:

- Assessment is ongoing, varied in nature, and administered over a period of time to provide multiple opportunities for students to demonstrate the full range of their learning
- The teacher provides ongoing descriptive feedback that is clear, specific, meaningful, and timely to support improved learning and achievement

(Ontario Ministry of Education, 2010)

The two main types of assessment used in checks for understanding are *assessment for learning* and *assessment as learning*.

Assessment *For* Learning

Assessment for learning is defined as "the frequent, interactive checking of student progress and understanding in order to identify learning needs and adjust teaching appropriately" (Younglove, 2011).

Assessment opportunities are everywhere in the classroom. Every observation the teacher or student makes, every conversation students engage in, and every product students complete or create are opportunities for assessment and feedback. Assessment is not about making sure tasks are completed (unless the goal is task completion); it is more often about knowing where students are in their learning in relation to the learning goal and success criteria, and what feedback will move students ahead in their learning.

Assessment *As* Learning

Assessment as learning is defined as the process of developing and supporting students to actively engage in the assessment process: that is, they monitor their own learning; use assessment feedback from teacher, self, and peers to determine next steps; and set individual learning goals. Assessment as learning requires students to have a clear understanding of the learning goals and the success criteria (Ontario Ministry of Education, 2010). Ideally, at the beginning of any lesson or unit, teachers and students will

- Assess the student's current level of knowledge or skill, in order to facilitate checks for understanding during the upcoming lesson
- Share, discuss, or co-construct the learning goals and success criteria for any particular lesson

This part of the lesson is the perfect time for students to be partners in understanding, assessing, and adjusting their practice to support their own learning. Here is an example of how to present learning goals and success criteria, so that students can participate in self-assessment/assessment as learning. This format can be used by the teacher and shared with students for every math unit.

Unit: Ratios and Percentages
Name: _____

Learning Goal	Success Criteria	Self-assessment	Next steps for my own learning
I can convert between fractions, percent, and decimals in order to improve my financial literacy.	I CAN… • convert a percent into a decimal by dividing by 100. • convert a decimal into a percent by multiplying by 100. • convert a fraction into a decimal by dividing the numerator by the denominator and apply this knowledge to real world shopping situations, both in person and online Other success criteria: Initialed by teacher: _____	I already knew how to _____ I feel confident with _____ I need extra practice with _____	

Assessments or checks for understanding throughout the lesson would measure students' growth in learning and consider next steps. During this time in the lesson, teacher and student can assess growth according to the stated goals and criteria, and measure growth from a baseline. As well, in the section on success criteria, there is a space for students to fill in their own success criteria, based on their understanding of the goal. There is a space for the teacher to initial the sheet, as an opportunity to check in on student-generated success criteria.

Feedback

Throughout this chapter and throughout the book, feedback is referenced as a way of giving information to students that supports learning. There are a number of different types of feedback, and all are important at certain points in the lesson.

Type of Feedback	Examples	Best if...	Effect
Motivational Feedback	"Well done." "Good for you." "I really like the way you are trying."	...focused on the task, not the learner.	This type of feedback affects self-concept and perceptions about motivation and intelligence, and so should be used carefully.
Evaluative Feedback	Marks, Percentages, Summative comments	...given at the end of a feedback cycle. ...not the only type of feedback for learning.	Clarity about overall achievement at the end of a learning cycle
Descriptive Feedback	Information about current achievement in relation to a goal and success criteria	...shared with students as strengths/next steps.	If focused on the task and structured effectively, it can support students to improve learning and achievement.

Descriptive feedback linked specifically to the learning goals and success criteria is a powerful tool for improving student learning and is fundamental to building a culture of learning within the classroom. Teacher, peers, and student provide feedback, and time is given for the student to respond to feedback prior to evaluation. The focus of the feedback is to encourage students to produce their best work by building on strengths and understanding next steps for improving upon their previous work.

Content Knowledge/Skill Checks for Understanding

There are three main ways that teachers and students can check in and collect data that informs teaching and learning, and these occur at many times throughout the lesson. These are checks through observations, conversations, and products.

It should be clear to students and teachers alike what they are checking for when they are assessing learning formatively.

- Observations can include small-group discussions, butterfly conferences (listening in briefly to a larger number of students as they read), content-focused discussions, oral retellings, oral rehearsal, instructional activities.
- Conversations can include conferencing (one-on-one), small-group discussions, butterfly conferences (listening in briefly to a larger number of students as they read), questioning/prompting dialogues.
- Products (examples) include reading conferences, a wide variety of writing products, graphic organizers, writing with prompts, free-writing, performances, inventions.

Observations

Observations involve the process of objectively watching something or someone carefully in order to gain information. Observations occur throughout the whole lesson; you observe engagement, behavior, and learning throughout the day. Part of the challenge is to know where to focus the multitude of observations in order to give the feedback necessary to move students along in their learning. Many teachers find note-taking during this portion of the lesson quite cumbersome. There are a variety of simple observation forms you can use.

SAMPLE CHECKS FOR UNDERSTANDING TEACHER OBSERVATION FORM:
GRADE 6 READING

Learning Goal: *I am able to select evidence from text that supports my point of view, in order to justify my opinions.*
Success Criteria:
- *I have a clear, strong point of view that I can articulate.*
- *I can reference facts and information from text.*
- *I can check the validity of the text I am using.*

Date	Student	Observed strengths in relation to the learning goal	Next steps for and articulated by student	Next steps for and articulated by teacher

March 8, 2018	Samara	• Can state a clear point of view after reading • Needs instruction to verify validity of sources	I want to figure out ways to know if the text I am reading comes from a valid author or website	• Guided instruction about critical literacy • Checking sources (checkology)

The key is for both student and teacher to have the learning goal in mind when learning is observed. The focus must be on objective information. Teachers can jot down their observations in multiple ways:

- on paper or on a paper form
- digitally
- using checkmarks for goals reached
- making quick anecdotal notes, with a focus on next steps for teaching/learning

When observing student learning, teachers must shift focus away from behavior to

- Noticing strengths first. It's easy to notice needs first, but it is crucial to notice and praise strengths (what the student can do) before giving any next-steps feedback. If students can build on their strengths or on known information or skills, they have a better chance to improve. For example, if a basketball player already knows how to do a layup and does it very well, it's a small step to a slam dunk. However, if that player is still working on the layup, teaching the slam dunk will be frustrating for both the coach and the player.
- Next-steps feedback that will support learning. Through observation, you will notice needs/next steps; at this point, choose to give feedback that supports learning and is related to the learning goals.

In any observation, it is important to consider the following questions in order, focusing first on strengths, then on next steps, then on feedback that would support learning, and ending with a reflection on future teaching:

1. What does this student already know or what can they already do?
2. What does the student still need to learn?
3. What feedback would help this student?
4. What do I, as the teacher, need to do differently tomorrow to support this student?

Note that acting on the fourth question is an excellent way to build rapport.

Conversations

A conversation is defined online as "an informal interchange of thoughts, information, etc. by spoken words: oral communication between [people]." Typically, during every part of a lesson, teachers check for understanding with questions like, "Do you understand?" "Any questions?" or "Does that make sense?" These types of prompts do not usually encourage conversation. Issues arise when teachers rely too heavily on these well-used questions and prompts to check in. When these questions are presented to the whole class or even in a small group, the majority of students

- Don't want to respond in front of peers if the content or new learning doesn't make sense or if they don't understand, because they don't want to look "stupid", especially as they get older.
- Don't participate; participation comes from a few students at best.
- Fake understanding to preserve their self-respect in front of peers.
- Can't think of their own questions when asked on the spot, but questions will arise as they practice.
- Are silent or nod, or both; these can be taken as a signs of understanding, when often they are not.

One example of an instructional activity is 4 Corners: students are given four options, decide which corner to go to based on their opinions, and then discuss their choice with others in their corner.

Conversations are not intended to be question-and-answer sessions. All too often, typical interactions in classrooms involve teachers trying to initiate a conversation by asking questions, students answering or responding to the questions, and teachers evaluating the answers and, in some cases, providing evaluative feedback; e.g., "Right," "Not quite," "Excellent." This is called the IRE (Initiation/ Response/Evaluation) paradigm, and in most cases it is not supportive of learning. In contrast, conversations need to be dialogues, and dialogues too often are not common practice in classrooms between students and teachers. In dialogues, teachers or peers can listen to student thinking without judgment or evaluation. It is important to decrease questioning and evaluative comments and increase conversations in order to truly check for understanding and support learning through talk.

Peter Johnston (2012) supports the notion of conversation through a dialogic approach. He states that oral text (or talk) is a crucially important part of teaching and learning. *Dialogic teaching* means using talk most effectively for carrying out teaching and learning. The dialogic approach will immediately change the way students relate to each other and expand their learning based on prompts for dialogue and deep thinking.

Through dialogue, teachers can elicit students' everyday, common-sense perspectives, engage with their developing ideas, and help overcome their misunderstandings. When students are given opportunities to contribute to classroom dialogue, their thinking is extended in varied ways, so they can explore the limits of their own understanding. At the same time, they practice new ways of using language as a tool for constructing knowledge. A dialogic approach creates

- more symmetrical power relationships between students and teacher
- language that encourages mutual engagement
- comfort with uncertainty
- focus on meaning-making
- multiple perspectives/a range of answers

Instead of relying on evaluative feedback such as "Good," "Excellent," "Not quite," or "Correct," try open-ended questions that encourage dialogue. The following prompts, to be used by teachers and students, encourage students to think more deeply and truly respond to one another in conversations:

- Can you tell me more about your thinking?
- What in the text made you think this?
- What do others think about _____'s idea?
- Can anyone add to _____'s thinking?
- Do agree or disagree with _____'s idea? Why?
- What questions would you like to ask _____?
- Would anyone like to add to what _____ said?
- What is an example of that?

In this type of conversation, the responses to student responses also change somewhat. Instead of (or in addition to) simple motivational feedback, such as "Good work," or "Well done," try non-evaluative responses:

"Thank you."
"Got it."
"I appreciate that."
"Were you right? How do you know?"

Checks for understanding are more powerful using talk as the medium. Resnick and her associates (Resnick et al., 2015) developed the concept of accountable talk. These are basically the agreements for all members of the classroom who agree to shared expectations for communicating about learning. Accountable talk is important for all interactions in the classroom: guided instruction, whole-class interactions, and partner or small-group student-moderated discussion.

There are five indicators of accountable talk:

1. Ask for clarification: "Can you further describe/explain what you mean?"
2. Ask for justification for proposals: "Where did you find that information?"
3. Recognize and challenge misconceptions: "Are you sure? I don't agree because..."
4. Ask for evidence for claims: "Can you give an example?"
5. Interpret and use other's statements: "Sarah suggested..."

Conversations or dialogue that include accountable talk are a wonderful way for teachers who listen in on conversations to decide on instructional next steps.

Products

Products are what is created, completed, or produced by the student. Teachers are sometimes tempted to evaluate products during practice time, making a judgment about whether or not the student learned the material (or completed the task) from the product. Instead, make the assessment formative (rather than evaluative) by prompting the student to assess their own product based on learning goals and success criteria. As an alternative, you can leave this time as a chance to give feedback. When you look at a product during the lesson or independent practice time, hold back judgment and instead check for understanding and clarify where the student is in their learning. Again, think of coaching an athlete just before they are ready for the game, at practices during the week prior

Shift away from question–answer formats or the IRE paradigm to conversations or dialogue in the classroom and monitor how to respond and give feedback to student thinking during conversations to make checks for understanding more detailed and effective.

Notice there is no place for evaluation in the accountable talk model.

101

to the game or even on the same day as the game. Once the game is played, the evaluation is summative. But everything leading up to the game (or final product) is an opportunity for formative feedback.

Use this framework when looking at products:

Instead of…	Try…
Go back and finish #5. I asked you to complete the whole page.	What do you think your strengths were in this assignment? Where do you still need to practice?
If I marked this now, it would get a C. Check the rubric.	Let's mark this together on the rubric, based on your learning. Tell me one or two areas where you still need to improve.
I see you've got it. Good for you!	What did you learn from this work?

Tips for Checks for Understanding

Whenever you assess formatively, you must first have a baseline assessment of students' knowledge and skills. For example, if a Grade 2 student began a fractions unit with a good understanding of ½ and whole, then that is the baseline. Here is the learning goal:

See page 53 for more on this example.

We are learning to recognize fractions (½, ¼, ⅓) in order to apply the learning to real-world problems like sharing food and understanding money.

When checking for understanding:

- Compare student learning to the established criteria, not to other students.
- Observe the student during whole-class, guided, and independent practice. For example, you might notice that the student can always complete the questions involving ½ and whole, and is showing some understanding of ¼ when using manipulatives to break up a whole and reconstruct it.
- Look at products together with the student, reflecting on learning goals and success criteria, consolidating strengths, and deciding together on next steps for learning. Checks for understanding and assessment for/as learning happen in context of growth toward the aspects of the goal that were not previously learned.
- Prompt for quality of student work over quantity. This can be challenging because it is counter-intuitive. Instead of noticing the amount of work completed, notice the learning represented in the work completed and comment or prompt for that:

  You've already completed the first question and shown you know how to split a whole into thirds.

You've split this pie into fractions, representing ⅓, or 3 parts of a whole. Try it again, splitting it into quarters, which means 4 parts of whole.
Once you understand ¼, you'll have figured out all the parts of our learning goal.

- Have a conversation with the student using questions/prompts that require elaboration, rather than short answers: *Can you tell me about your thinking? What else do you know? Let's look at our success criteria and see where you are at in your learning.*

    "I wonder what would happen if we had four people and they each wanted a part. What do you think?"

- Incorporate dialogue when checking for understanding. The moment we ask a student a question about their work, they think they are wrong. (Try it and you'll see.) If you ask a student, *How did you get this answer?* or *What else could you have tried?*, they infer that the work is incorrect. Instead, encourage dialogue and opportunities for formative assessment by using prompts like these:

    - *This makes sense to me. Tell me about this response.*
    - *I agree with this. How did you know?*
    - *I disagree with this. Am I right or are you right?*
    - *Your way makes sense. I wonder if it also makes sense this way.*

It is tempting to think comments like "Johnny is almost finished, and you've only done two questions" are motivating. However, instead of achieving the desired result of motivating students to get started or work faster, it embarrasses students; it might make them feel overwhelmed. Above all, it negatively affects your rapport with the student. Instead, avoid using references to other students and their work: *You've started the first question. Let's see what you already know. Let's read the success criteria together and you can describe for me what skills you'll need for the next section.*

    "We're working on three different types of fractions. I'd like to see a sample of all three. So far, you clearly understand ½, so let's try the others."

Silent Responses

Sometimes, you need feedback from students about their own understanding during a small-group or whole-class part of the lesson, in order to guide instruction. One easy way to get this information is through silent responses. Response cards provide a variety of different ways that students in the group can share their own understanding at the same time in response to a question or problem posed by the teacher or another student. They also allow for full participation by every member of the group or class. There are different formats for silent responses using response cards:

Thumbs Up/Thumbs Down/Thumbs to the Side

In this format, students share one of the different options to indicate understanding. Thumbs up means *Yes, I understand.* Thumbs down means *No, I don't yet understand.* Thumbs to the side means *I understand some of this.* You can do a quick scan to see how many students and which individual students fall into each category. But remember, as it is a public response, there might still be times when students don't want to give honest feedback in front of peers.

Index Cards

Printed cards can give a few possible response options to students. Students would each be given a *Yes* card and a *No* card to hold up. Be careful to ask only questions that can be answered with a Yes/No response, such as predictions or literal comprehension questions. This type of response format does not work particularly well for thinking questions, so you might want to pair students for a discussion after they have responded to a simple question. For example, if you are using the book *Wishtree* by Katherine Applegate, a beautiful book about a centuries-old tree that tells wonderful stories, questions like the following should lead to discussion:

> *Do you think Red (the oak tree) has any special gifts?*
> *Do you believe that Samar and Stephen will be friends?*
> *Does Red like being the wishtree?*

Stop/Go cards (either separate Stop and Go or two-sided cards) allow each student to hold up the card when they need you to stop and re-explain. As well, you can stop at strategic points and ask students to hold up the Go card if you can continue teaching or put up the Stop card if you need to re-explain content or process. It is important to be willing to respond to these messages by students if you ask for the feedback.

You or students can print opposite responses on two cards (or back to back). For example:

Mixed Number/Improper Fraction for Math
Amphibian/Reptile for Science
True/False for any fact-based lesson

Digital Responses

Check out Google Forms for a wide range of forms, some specifically for education.

Students are given an opportunity to respond in any of the ways we've discussed to a question or problem posed, but digitally, and in real time. The information can be collected immediately and displayed for the class. The data can be displayed anonymously for the class, but you can see which students responded by demonstrating understanding and which require more support/instruction. Many apps are available; even Google Classroom templates allow students to respond in this way.

Strategies for Teachers and Students to Check for Understanding

Here are some strategies to replace the all too familiar "how's it going?" approach to checks for understanding. These strategies incorporate observations, conversations, and products, combined with appropriate motivational and descriptive feedback to encourage rapport, to check in on learning. In just a short time (10 minutes), you can check in with a few students. As well, students can check in on themselves to see how they are learning in relation to the stated goals.

Check-In Prompts

The teacher or a peer can prompt a student with one or more of these questions. Practice in small groups first, so students know the expectations for asking and responding to these types of questions.

For the third and fourth questions, students will be more willing to respond honestly if their rapport with teacher and peers is positive.

- *What are you learning?*
- *How are you doing? How do you know?*
- *What do you still need in order to be successful/to improve?*
- *How can I help?*

Sticky Notes

I am a big fan of sticky notes. Here are some of the reasons:

- They vary by color and size, so they can be used for different purposes, such as sharing an idea, making a longer note, asking a question, jotting down a wondering, or making a quick comment.
- They can be easily grouped and re-grouped, depending on the purpose.
- Once a student has put their thinking on a sticky note, it gives them an opportunity to get up and post it (move) somewhere.
- They help teachers hear and value student voice at various points in the lesson.
- Different-colored notes can signal different types of feedback; for example, motivational feedback (given by teachers or peers) can be on yellow notes and descriptive feedback can be on purple notes.
- They can be passed around easily, discussed and re-sorted, or posted after being checked or discussed.
- They can be anonymous or not.
- They can be posted on anchor charts and used over the course of many lessons.
- They don't need to be permanent records of learning; therefore, they work well for formative assessment.

For example, you can assign a color to each of the following prompts:

- *Jot a question you have.*
- *Jot one idea that wasn't mentioned.*
- *Write down an "I wonder" if you have one.*

Then ask students to pass it to a peer who chose the same color for a brief conversation, or post it in the appropriate column on the class chart.

SAMPLE STICKY NOTE CHECK-IN: GRADE 5

Lesson: Free Verse Poetry from the Heart Learning Goal: We are learning the form of free verse poetry, which is one of the literary genres and a new way to express feelings and thoughts.		
Questions we have?	One idea that wasn't mentioned	I wonder...

What makes a poem free verse?	*Let's do a free verse poem based on the sport we like best.*	*Is rap free verse?*

If the note is shared with a peer first, the peer can jot a quick response (agree, disagree, tell me more, thumbs up, thumbs down) on the note before sharing it with a larger group or the whole class. With this approach, you get a lot of formative assessment information and a clearer understanding of student interests when checking for understanding.

Check-In Tickets

These are typically given to students when they arrive to class (to check in on what they still remember from the last class) or at the end of class (to check in on what they learned during the class and what still needs to be re-explained or retaught). As with any whole-class check-in, you will receive a wide range of responses to the same questions and have to decide what to do with the information: Reteach because 30% of the kids didn't learn it? Try a guided approach next class? Move on because 70% of kids learned it? Assign more practice? Instead of thinking of the check-ins as a whole-class barometer for learning, think of each student individually as you check in on learning.

- Take the first five minutes of class to review tickets-out-the-door with some students. This allows you to quickly conference with individual students who had questions or misunderstandings at the end of last class, and to make the learning in the upcoming lesson more meaningful. Create a dialogue with prompts that support a conversation to focus on the misunderstandings and clarify the goal for learning, giving some responsibility to the student to assess what they need to do next.

    I noticed here that you wrote you didn't understand the lesson. Which part of the lesson was challenging?
    Let's review the goal together. What part do you understand?
    Let's review your practice work together. Where do you see strengths in your learnings?
    I can re-explain it and then let's see if it's clearer.
    Would more practice help?

- Take the first five minutes of class to set up a quick peer conference for some students. Put a student's ticket on the desk of a peer, who then finds the student and has a quick discussion about it. For example, if a student wrote: *I'm not sure how to demonstrate the success criteria for #4* and another student clearly does, those two students can be paired. The conference can be two-way (each shares their ticket from the last check-in and responds to the other) or one-way (the peer supports the learning of their classmate). Rapport, again, is crucial in this type of conference or check-in.

- Give choice. Allow students to choose their ticket-in/out-the-door from among a few options:

3-2-1 Exit Ticket
Name: _____
3 things that you learned today.
2 interesting things.
1 question you still have.

What/Why/When?
What was the learning goal from today?

Why are we learning this?

When will you ever use this in real life?

But What About…
One thing I still don't think I understand:

How will I demonstrate? (fill in success criteria here)

Who would be more helpful in reviewing this with me?
Peer   Teacher

At the beginning of the next class, group students who chose similar exit tickets, so they can discuss their common learning strengths and needs.

- **Have students imagine the quiz.** In the middle or at the end of the lesson, give students five minutes to write two or three questions that would assess their understanding of the content of the lesson. The next day, ask the students to answer a few of the questions as a check-in.
- **Have students rate themselves on a scale of 1 to 5.** Ask students to choose one of the success criteria, look at the product of their work, and rate themselves between 1 (*I still don't get it*) and 5 (*I understand it all*) on that one area of learning. Then have students write down one next step for their own learning to be successful in that one area. See page 109 for an Self-Assessment template.

Google Forms are a great way to use technology to support checks for understanding. You can quickly create exit tickets, worksheets, or quick assessments that support learning. The information is gathered and shared through Google Classroom. These forms are very easy to use and give you a quick snapshot of learning from which to plan instructional next steps.

Sample Checks for Understanding
Teacher Observation Form

Learning Goal:

Success Criteria:

Date	Student	Observed strengths in relation to the learning goal	Next steps for and articulated by student	Next steps for and articulated by teacher

Pembroke Publishers © 2018 *Inspiring Meaningful Learning* by Brenda Stein Dzaldov ISBN 978-1-55138-334-7

Self-Assessment Form

Product	Success criteria I am checking on	My rating from 1 to 5 1: *I still don't get it* 5: *I understand it all*	Next step for my own learning

Pembroke Publishers © 2018 *Inspiring Meaningful Learning* by Brenda Stein Dzaldov ISBN 978-1-55138-334-7

7

Closing the Lesson

"What gives anyone the right to take 3 away from 8?
Why should 8 be diminished to the lesser value of
5 just to satisfy someone's obsession with math?"

DESIGNING THE SIXTH STEP

Closure (5 minutes)	☐ Lesson review and wrap-up/Reflection ☐ Recording of homework, important information ☐ Closure question/prompt (to spark curiosity for next lesson) ☐ Appreciations

Lesson Closure

Closure is the point in the lesson where students have a moment to reflect on learning, ask a final question (probably one that will need to be addressed during the next lesson), perhaps complete a ticket out the door, and say thank you or goodbye for the day. Closure is sometimes the part of the lesson that is missed. As time is often short, teachers will quickly move from subject to subject or task to task without providing closure for the lesson at hand.

> **CLOSURE: SOUP EXAMPLE**
>
> If you spend an hour making a pot of soup, you probably want to serve it. You have to decide whether you will keep the pot boiling for another 30 minutes or turn it off to cool. You have to make a quick plan about how much to freeze, how much you will keep in the refrigerator after cooling, and how much will be served today. You can't just walk away from what you have created or learned. In some sense, the same is true at school.

Since the closure portion of the lesson is just five minutes, you have a very short amount of time to give students a chance to reflect on their learning, do a self-assessment, record salient information, summarize learning by responding to a closure question or prompt in preparation for the next lesson, or take a moment to say something positive to peers or receive positive feedback in the form of appreciations. There won't be time to do all of these activities, so choose a closure activity that makes sense for that lesson or series of lessons.

Lesson Review and Wrap-up/Reflection

Closing the lesson usually requires a quick summary of what was learned as you let students know that the lesson is coming to a close. Students can participate by sharing ideas for the ways their learning met their learning goals.

SAMPLE LESSON REVIEWS

	Learning Goal	Summary of what was learned
Grade 2 Social Studies	*I am learning about the people in my community.*	*Today, we learned about helpers in our community, such as doctors, firefighters, and ambulance drivers.*

Grade 6 Science	*We are learning to design and safely build parallel and series circuits.*	*Today, we learned that there are two kinds of ways to connect circuits. We practiced looking at series circuits, where the current that flows through each part of the circuit is the same. The current from a switch to a lightbulb is a series circuit.*
Grade 8 Math	*We are learning about the angles in a triangle and the relationships between them.*	*Today, we learned that sum of all angles in a triangle must equal 180 degrees. This helps us understand how triangles are solid 2-D shapes and the building blocks of many different structures.*

Approaches to summary/reflection:

1. Simply remind students what they learned today. You may choose to highlight interesting comments or progress (e.g., "Remember when Sumaya discovered that…") and consolidate the *why* of learning. This will create an environment where students leave the lesson feeling that something was accomplished and that there was meaning in their time spent in class.

See page 117 for a Ponder That Quote template.

PONDER THAT QUOTE

One great way to do this is through a closure activity called Ponder That Quote: choose three or four quotes directly related to the lesson (or have students do this part as an extension to the lesson). Have students choose a quote and a respond to it. This can be done in pairs, in small groups, or with the whole class. Responses can take several forms:

- Explain it (to a friend, to your group, to the class)
- Make a personal connection to the quote
- Tell us something you like (or don't like) about it
- Share a question you have about it

> *Narrative writing must tell a story in such a way that the audience learns a life lesson.*
> *Narrative writing includes a theme, characters, plot, and setting.*
> *Your experiences inform your narrative writing.*
> *Novels, short stories, comics, plays, musicals, and poetry can all be narratives.*
> Choose a quote. Respond to it in one of the following ways (your choice):
> 1. Explain it (to a friend/to your group/to the class) using your own examples.
> 2. Make a personal connection to the quote.
> 3. Tell us something you agree with or don't agree with and why.
> 4. Share a question you have about the quote.

2. Ask students to respond orally or in writing to one of these prompts, to encourage consolidation and reflection:

   Today, I/we learned…because…
   Today's learning was important to me/us…because…

This can be done as a whole class, in small groups, in pairs, or even individually as students jot their responses on paper or on a digital platform. Students will become familiar with these prompts over time.

3. Give students a final opportunity to ask a question or share a wondering, orally or in writing. This can guide your own teaching for the next class:

   I still have a question, and it's…
   I was wondering…

   Students can write questions and wonderings on sticky notes and share them anonymously. They can put their names on the questions/wonderings, which can lead to further discussion if necessary.

4. A ticket-out-the-door is a quick way to have students give feedback and to contextualize their learning. For example, you can use a What?/So What?/Now What? organizer. The *What?* reviews content. The *So What?* reviews context; i.e., why we are learning this. The *Now What?* sparks students to think about what is next.

See page 118 for a What?/So What?/Now What? Ticket-Out-the-Door template.

SAMPLE WHAT?/SO WHAT?/NOW WHAT? TICKETS-OUT-THE-DOOR

	What?	So What?	Now What?
Grade 6 Science	*We learned about parallel and series circuits.*	*It's important to understand this when thinking about any flow of electricity.*	*I'm thinking of creating a series circuit to light up a purple lightbulb!*

Grade 8 Math	We learned about the sum of angles in triangles.	If we know it always adds up to 180 degrees, then we can simply calculate the angles in any triangle.	We will soon have a chance to build a structure using triangles, so we need to know about this so our structure is steady!

A ticket-out-the-door for closure can allow students to share whether they understood the concepts taught or need more instruction. Students write the learning goal (or their version of it), and then choose a card between

See page 119 for Stop/Start/Continue Ticket-Out-the-Door templates.

- *STOP!* for parts of the lesson that confused the student
- *START!* for ideas to explore next
- *CONTINUE!* for further clarification

Recording of Homework/Important Information

This is often another challenging part at the end of a lesson. Some students have completed their practice and don't have any homework, so those students have nothing to record. Other students are slow at writing down information. Still others don't take responsibility to record homework. Some students require a scribe to get the information written down.

Technology is changing this part of the lesson for teachers. The easiest way to make sure everyone has the same basic information is to post it on a class blog, Moodle, or classroom site. It can take the form of

- a photo of the assigned task or of an exemplar shared in class, accompanied by brief summary
- an upload of an anchor chart or slides used during the lesson
- the posting of a video of yourself or a student explaining important information

If this step is planned, time doesn't run out at the end of a lesson to get down important, required information. Students can be expected to check in to the classroom site or blog at some point after the lesson ends to get the information needed.

Closure Question/Prompt

In order both to make learning meaningful and to set students up for the next lesson, it's a great idea to spark curiosity for the next lesson. Let students know what is coming up for them by

- showing them a picture that will inform learning for the next class
- telling them about upcoming learning activities
- telling them what the first five minutes of next class will look like
- telling them to expect a puzzle, picture, or guiding question at the beginning of next class

Remember, closure is not so much an end point, as a final check-in.

- asking them to share one question they still have about what was learned; if you have time, you can share a couple of the most interesting questions

Appreciations

Appreciations are a final way to build rapport during the lesson. Rapport is built when you show

- care about students and their learning
- awareness about student needs and interests
- enthusiasm toward learning
- that students are treated with fairness and equity

This is the opportunity to thank students for their attention and commitment to learning that day:

Thank you for your commitment to learning today.
It was great to see you follow your interests and write about _____ today.
I was excited to watch the small-group work and see how you helped each other reach your goals.

You might even ask a few students to appreciate each other for something that happened in class:

- Ask students to speak to a classmate by name, telling them something they appreciated today.
- Make an appreciation statement about learning, and ask students to give a thumbs-up if they agree.

Some authentic statements from the prompts could include the following:

"We appreciate when Sam asked a good question and helped clarify for us."
"We appreciate the collaboration in the groups, which helped us move closer to the learning goal today."
"We appreciate the peer feedback given that clarified the success criteria and helped us learn."
"It was great to have the opportunity to build structures together today!"

Taking a moment to revisit what makes rapport an important part of learning is worthwhile, for you and for your students. Your appreciations at the end of the lesson can reflect that.

Goodbye to Students

Be sure to say goodbye to your students, just as you welcomed them into learning, and let them know that you are looking forward to seeing them the next day. When you close the class on a note of praise, positive feedback, or a kind word, students feel good about their learning experience.

Ponder That Quote

Choose one of the quotes above. Respond to it in one of the following ways (your choice):

1. Explain it (to a friend/to your group/to the class) using your own examples.

2. Make a personal connection to the quote.

3. Tell us something you agree with or don't agree with and why.

4. Share a question that you have about the quote.

What?/So What?/Now What? Ticket-out-the-Door

What?	So What?	Now What?

Pembroke Publishers © 2018 *Inspiring Meaningful Learning* by Brenda Stein Dzaldov ISBN 978-1-55138-334-7

Stop/Start/Continue Ticket-Out-the-Door

Learning Goal:

STOP! These are the parts of the lesson that confused me:

Learning Goal:

START! I have an idea we could explore next:

Learning Goal:

CONTINUE! I could still use some clarification on this:

Acknowledgments

To Mary Macchuisi and Kat Mototsune, for your support and for giving me the opportunity to share my experiences and love of teaching and learning with others.

To those friends and colleagues who have encouraged me throughout my career. Kind words and kind deeds have pushed me forward each day, and I don't take any of them for granted. Thank you for your simple kindness.

To all of my contributors, and to the teachers and students who willingly share their thoughts, reflections, experiences, and expertise with me as we travel on this educational journey together. Thank you.

Professional Resources

Andrade, H. (2010) "Students as the Definitive Source of Formative Assessment: Academic self-assessment and the self-regulation of learning" In H. L. Andrade and G. J. Cizek (Eds.), *Handbook of Formative Assessment* (pp. 233–250). New York, NY: Routledge.

Bennett, B., & Rolheiser, C. (2001) *Beyond Monet: The artful science of instructional integration.* Toronto, ON: Bookation.

Black, P., Harrison, C., Lee, C., Marshall, B., & Wiliam, D. (2004) "Working Inside the Black Box: Assessment for learning in the classroom" *Phi Delta Kappan*, 86(1), 9–21.

Black, P., Harrison, C., Lee, C., & Wiliam, D. (2003) *Assessment for Learning: Putting it into practice.* New York, NY: Open University Press.

Booth, D. (2008) *It's Critical: Classroom strategies for promoting critical and creative comprehension.* Markham, ON: Pembroke.

Bransford, J., Brown, A., & Cocking, R. (Eds.) (2000) *How People Learn: Brain, mind, experience, and school.* Washington DC: National Academy Press [National Research Council].

Brookhart, S. M. (2008) *How to Give Effective Feedback to Your Students.* Alexandria, VA: Association for Supervision and Curriculum Development.

Buckner, A. (2005) *Notebook Know-How: Strategies for the writer's notebook.* Portland, ME: Stenhouse.

Butler, D., & Cartier, S. (2004) "Promoting Effective Task Interpretation as an Important Work Habit: A key to successful teaching and learning" *Teachers College Record*, 106(9), 1729–1758.

Chappuis, J. (2009) *Seven Strategies of Assessment for Learning.* Portland, OR: Educational Testing Service.

Chappuis, S., & Stiggins, R. (2002) "Classroom Assessment for Learning" *Educational Leadership*, 60(1), 40–43.

Charney, Ruth (2002) *Teaching Children to Care: Classroom management for ethical and academic growth, K–8.* Turners Falls, MA: Northeast Foundation for Children.

Clarke, S. (2008) *Active Learning through Formative Assessment.* London, UK: Hodder Education.

Costa, A., & Kallick, B. (1993) "Through the Lens of a Critical Friend" *Educational Leadership*, 51(2), 49–55.

Csikszentmihalyi, Michaly (2000) "Finding Flow: The psychology of engagement with everyday life" *Journal of Happiness Studies*, 1(1), 121–123.

Dirksen, Debra (2001) "Hitting the Reset Button: Using formative assessment to guide instruction" *Phi Delta Kappan*, 92(7), 26-31.

Dweck, Carol (2006) *Mindset: The new psychology of success.* New York, NY: Random House.

Fletcher, R. (2010) *A Writer's Notebook: Unlocking the writer within you.* Kindle Edition. New York, NY: Harper Collins.

Fraser, S. (2011) *Authentic Childhood: Experiencing Reggio Emilia in the classroom, 3rd Edition.* Toronto, ON: Nelson Education.

Fredericks, J. A., Blumenfeld, P. C., & Paris, A. H. (2004) "School Engagement: Potential of the concept, state of the evidence" *Review of Educational Research*, 74, 59–109.

Hattie, J. (2012) *Visible Learning for Teachers: Maximizing impact on learning.* New York, NY: Routledge.

Hattie, J., & Yates, G. (2014) *Visible Learning and the Science of How We Learn.* New York, NY: Routledge.

Hattie, J. & Timperley, H. (2007) "The Power of Feedback" *Review of Educational Research*, 77(1), 81–112.

Horn, M., & Giacobbe, M. E. (2007) *Talking, Drawing, Writing: Lessons for our youngest writers.* Portland, ME: Stenhouse.

Johnston, Peter (2004) *Choice Words: How our language affects children's learning.* Portland, ME: Stenhouse.

Johnston, Peter (2012) *Opening minds: How classroom talk shapes children's minds and their lives.* Portland, ME: Stenhouse.

Martin-Kniep, G., & Picone-Zocchia, J. (2009) *Changing the Way You Teach: Improving the way students learn.* Alexandria, VA: Association for Supervision and Curriculum Development.

Moss, C., & Brookhart, S. (2009) *Advancing Formative Assessment in Every Classroom: A guide for instructional leaders.* Alexandria, VA: Association for Supervision and Curriculum Development.

Nicol, D., & Macfarlane-Dick, D. (2006) "Formative Assessment and Self-regulated Learning: A model and seven principles of good feedback practice" *Studies in Higher Education*, 31(2), 199– 218.

Nichols, Maria (2006) *Comprehension Through Conversation.* Portsmouth, NH: Heinemann.

Ontario Ministry of Education (2010) *Growing Success: Assessment, evaluation, and reporting in Ontario schools. First edition, covering Grades 1 to 12.* Toronto, ON: Ontario Ministry of Education.

Ontario Ministry of Education Monograph (2012) "The Third Teacher" Capacity Building Series, 27. Retrieved at http://www.edu.gov.on.ca/eng/literacynumeracy/inspire/research/CBS_ThirdTeacher.pdf.

Pearson, P. D. & Gallagher, M.C. (1983) "The Instruction of Reading Comprehension" *Contemporary Educational Psychology*, 8, 317–344.

Popham, W. J. (2008) *Transformative Assessment.* Alexandria, VA: Association for Supervision and Curriculum Development.

Ray, K. W., & Glover, M. (2008) *Already Ready: Nurturing writers in preschool and kindergarten.* Portsmouth, NH: Heinemann.

Resnick, L.B., Asterhan, C.S.C., & Clarke, S.N. (Eds.) (2015) *Socializing Intelligence through Academic Talk and Dialogue.* Washington, DC: American Educational Research Association.

Rolheiser, C., & Ross, J. A. (2001) "Student Self-evaluation: What research says and what practice shows" in R. D. Small and A. Thomas (Eds.), *Plain Talk about Kids* (pp. 43–57). Covington, LA: Centre for Development and Learning.

Russell, D. & Hunter, M. (1976) *Planning for Effective Instruction Lesson Design.* Los Angeles, CA: Seeds Elementary School.

Sadler, D. (1989) "Formative Assessment and the Design of Instructional Systems" *Instructional Science*, 18, 119–144.

Shepard, L., Hammerness, K., Darling-Hammond, L., Rust, F., Baratz Snowden, J., Gordon, E., Gutierrez, C., & Pacheco, A. (2005) "Assessment" in L. Darling-Hammond and J. Bransford (Eds.), *Preparing Teachers for a Changing World: What teachers should learn and be able to do* (pp. 275–326). San Francisco, CA: Jossey-Bass.

Shepard, L. (2006) "Classroom Assessment" in R. L. Brennan (Ed.), *Educational Measurement* (4th ed., 623–646). Westport, CT: Praeger.

Shulman, L. (1986) "Those Who Understand: Knowledge growth in teaching" *Educational Researcher*, 15(2), 4–14.

Stead, T. (2009) *Good Choice! Supporting independent reading and response, K–6.* Portland, ME: Stenhouse.

Stiggins, R. (2010) "Essential formative assessment competencies for teachers and school leaders" in H. L. Andrade and G. J. Cizek (Eds.), *Handbook of Formative Assessment* (pp. 233–250). New York, NY: Routledge.

Stiggins, R. J., Arter, J. A., *Chappuis, J., & Chappuis, S. (2006) Classroom Assessment for Student Learning: Doing it right—using it well.* Princeton, NJ: Educational Testing Service.

Stiggins, R. (2002) "Assessment Crisis: The absence of assessment FOR learning" *Phi Delta Kappan*, 83(10), 758–765.

Vygotsky, L. S. (1978) *Mind in Society: The development of higher psychological processes* (Cole, M., John-Steiner, V., Scribner, S. & Souberman, E., Eds.) Cambridge, MA.: Harvard University Press.

Woolfolk, A., Winne, P., & Perry, N. (2012) *Educational Psychology, Third custom edition.* Toronto, ON: Pearson.

Younglove, Bill (2011) "(In)Formative assessment: The key to accountability" *The Professional Journal of the California Association of Teachers of English* Vol. 17 (2), 21–23.

Internet Citations

https://www.youtube.com/watch?v=mBwf-VPZqDs
Video of "You are not alone", 2015

https://www.youtube.com/watch?v=Pu0uZUKSC-s
States of matter video

www.beebirch.com
Dana Chapman's Bee Birch Yoga Therapy

http://www.edugains.ca/newsite/aer/aervideo/learninggoals.html
Learning Goals and Success Criteria Video Library

https://www.youtube.com/watch?v=YUooOYbgSUg,
John Hattie speaking about inquiry learning

https://nationalgeographic.org
or https://kids.nationalgeographic.com
Definition, videos and other information about natural disasters

https://www.youtube.com/watch?v=ojiebVw8O0g
The flipped classroom

https://www.youtube.com/watch?v=K7ncXtZQSCg
Rachel Albert's One Point Perspective Video – The flipped classroom

https://www.youtube.com/channel/UCSUVCrhqUhbU4-BHvJeIOIA/
    feed?view_as=subscriber.
Teacher Rachel Albert's YouTube channel

https://www.pinterest.ca/sarahanneinoz/
    gradual-release-of-responsibility-model/?lp=true
The Optimal Learning Model

Index